EDRIC CANNON

THE POWER OF MENTAL DISCIPLINE

Master Your Mind, Achieve Your Goals, and Unlock Your Full Potential (2024 Beginner Guide)

Copyright © 2024 by Edric Cannon

All rights reserved. No part of this publication may be reproduced, stored or transmitted in any form or by any means, electronic, mechanical, photocopying, recording, scanning, or otherwise without written permission from the publisher. It is illegal to copy this book, post it to a website, or distribute it by any other means without permission.

First edition

This book was professionally typeset on Reedsy.
Find out more at reedsy.com

Contents

1	Chapter 1: The Power of Mental Discipline	1
2	Chapter 2:Self Belief	8
3	Chapter 3: Self-Belief and Weakness	17
4	Chapter 4: Mental Toughness	23
5	Chapter 5: Willpower	29
6	Chapter 6: Mastermind Planning	37
7	Chapter 7: Intelligence Versus Emotion	46
8	Chapter 8:Controlling the Mind	59
9	Chapter 9: Emotions, Fear, and Setbacks	70
10	Chapter 10: Overcoming Fears and Setbacks	82
11	PART 2	88
12	Chapter 11: How to Maximize Your Willpower	89
13	Chapter 12: Creating a Positive Self	98
14	Chapter 13: Hacking Your Way to Better Discipline	104
15	Chapter 14: Applying Your Discipline	113
16	Chapter 15: Boosting Your Efforts	128
17	Chapter 16: Defending Your Discipline	134
18	Outro	143

Chapter 1: The Power of Mental Discipline

POSITIVE PSYCHOLOGY COACHING SERIES

THE POWER OF MENTAL DISCIPLINE

A Practical Guide to Controlling Your Thoughts, Increasing Your Willpower and Achieving More

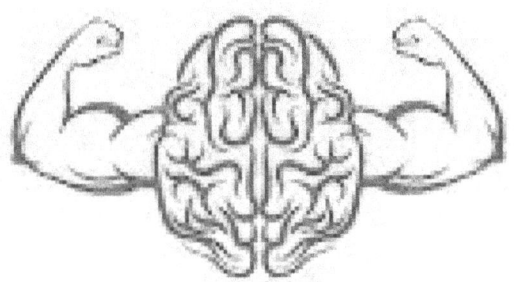

IAN TUHOVSKY

CHAPTER 1: THE POWER OF MENTAL DISCIPLINE

One quality we frequently hear about is mental discipline. You'll nearly always find it if you visit any inspirational social media page, read a book on attracting riches, love, or success, or go through any list of successful individuals. Words like "work hard," "don't stop," and "believe in yourself" will appear. These are the steps you must do, yet they are all related to one another. I've dedicated a significant amount of effort to addressing this area in my own life since those who served as my mentors ingrained it in me. I still clearly recall that moment when one of those mentors, a former special forces operative, spoke those words to me.

"Self-Discipline"

It is really succinct and straightforward, isn't it? What does that signify, though? The explanation was provided since the journalist was also curious. The precise words have been lost to time, but the idea was clear: self-motivation is having the capacity to drive oneself without assistance or guidance from others. It's the capacity to keep going and have faith when all else looks hopeless. It's the capacity to push oneself when no one else is looking, maintain optimism, and adjust to obstacles.

To put it briefly, discipline is the fundamental quality that underpins such abilities and will be important under stressful circumstances. Special forces troops are prepared to handle the worst-case scenarios and the highest levels of strain.

What Mental Discipline Means

A successful businessperson or athlete is frequently asked how they continue to push through obstacles in order to reach their objectives. We all aspire to live the lifestyles of the ultra-rich, after all. In actuality, most individuals don't consider the effort required to get there—rather, they only focus on the benefits.

Elon Musk is a prime illustration of this. With a net worth

of over $20 billion, he is extremely wealthy and well-known worldwide due to his inventive inventions. Moreover, he has been in relationships with young, incredibly stunning singers and actors over the past few years. Men abound who would relish these benefits, and women abound who would relish the reverse.

Musk maintained his high-risk strategy with a number of company launches, and he put in an absurd amount of effort to get to this point. Thirty years later, he continues to maintain a hectic schedule.

However, he reportedly made some cuts, working "easier" 90-hour work weeks.

Can you imagine how difficult it would be to get out of bed and start a 14-hour workday early in the morning if you had $20 billion, five children, and a really attractive girlfriend to see? Alternatively, to turn it up during crucial moments and start sleeping in your office to ensure that every second was dedicated to work?

All of this falls under the category of having the self-discipline and motivation to accomplish the tasks at hand. That might need extensive, rigorous practice when no one is around. It can include taking the initiative and planning on your own without other guidance. It may need you to dig deep to bear any degree of suffering as long as you keep going—just like the soldier from before would have done.

You see, the fundamental quality that drives the characteristics of successful individuals is mental discipline. It's the main reason successful individuals would put in extra effort even if they could just as easily give up and take their money. It's also the reason they can persevere and the motivation behind their drive to learn.

Effort Versus Talent

The main issue with a lot of individuals nowadays is that they think talent or luck are the main factors in success. It doesn't.

To begin with, luck is a random element. Naturally, a very small percentage of people will succeed only by accident. These are today's reality TV celebrities, lottery winners, and fortunate gamblers. Most of these folks won't experience long-term success.

For instance, lottery winners frequently experience financial ruin. This is a result of the fact that they were never taught how to manage money or the importance of the labor that would go into being wealthy. As a result, they frequently spend money and run out.

The hardships and hard work that so many accomplished individuals have endured help to shape their character. These folks now possess mental fortitude, a keen business sense, and the capacity to take measured risks because of them. It's the reason they cherish their achievements and have the self-control to manage their finances wisely. All of those challenging moments, which eventually had to be faced, are a portion of the true price of achievement.

Talent is comparable. It has the potential to be amazing. While many people possess some skill, success ultimately comes from discipline and hard effort. The common thread among most athletes is that they have worked really hard from an early age.

After receiving plaudits for their performance, one group was informed that their ratings could only have been attained by skill or intelligence. The other group received recognition for their diligence, which they were informed must have contributed to their success.

They were then offered the option to take a test that was

either harder or equally challenging. Most of the talented bunch decided to take an identical test. It is thought that this has to do with their assumption that their success is the result of natural skill. It would consequently be more difficult to receive the same score on a tougher test.

In the meantime, practically everyone of the second group decided to take the harder test.

Breaking Barriers

Belief is another way that mental discipline translates into accomplishment in the actual world. Many people have overcome incredibly restrictive conditions to become among the world's finest at what they do. Stephen Hawking is a prime illustration. Here is a brilliant individual, considered to be among the greatest brains of our day, who was also afflicted with ALS at the age of 21. It was said to him at the time that he would only have a few years left to live since his physical capabilities would quickly deteriorate. Stephen lived for a further 55 years after losing nearly all of his capacity to move or speak. During this period, he focused his thoughts on physics and developed several well accepted ideas.

Could he have accomplished this if he had given up and lost the will and self-control to go on? Not likely. Consider Roger Bannister, the first person to run a mile in under four minutes. Although it was thought to be impossible for centuries, Roger would declare from an early age that he would succeed, and he did. He surpassed the four-minute mark for the first time in history in 1954. It's not the story's most notable aspect that Bannister beat the clock. The fact that his record was surpassed a few months later and that three guys broke the four-minute barrier in a single race a year later is the problem! It's hardly even thought of as all that remarkable these days.

CHAPTER 1: THE POWER OF MENTAL DISCIPLINE

The same is true of the mental discipline effect. It's believing without wavering that something is possible and that you can accomplish it, even if it's not yet evident how the outcome will turn out.

You may refine this degree of discipline by forming a strong mental image and instilling the appropriate beliefs in your head. It may be used as a weapon, a component of your life's toolset, and to accomplish all of your goals.

But be aware that discipline is a difficult quality to acquire. It is straightforward since it lacks a great deal of complication. It does, however, need for daily and moment-by-moment effort and constancy.

2

Chapter 2: Self Belief

CHAPTER 2: SELF BELIEF

There are many large, stunning buildings in the world, some of which are constructed in a way that appears to be a feat of engineering. Constructions such as the Channel Tunnel and the Palm Islands in Dubai appear miraculous because, prior to their construction, most people would not have thought such concepts were feasible. This also applies to many other buildings, such as the International Space Station, the Large Hadron Collider, and the Burj Khalifa.

However, the origin of each of these works of art is the same: an idea. You undoubtedly already know that individuals all throughout the world develop ideas on a daily basis. Some people are dreadful, some are wonderful, some are bad, and some are somewhere in between. But the action performed is more important than the thought.

This is easy to do with certain ideas. It would be rather easy to implement your concept if it is to purchase product A and try to sell it to your friends. Regardless matter how basic the idea is, it still requires action, and a lot of individuals never take the necessary steps to make their ideas a reality.

What, then, enables certain people to take the necessary steps to realize their ideas? The solution is the same regardless of how straightforward or complex the concept seems. These individuals trust in themselves and their ideas!

You will take the necessary steps if you have a straightforward notion in which you have a strong belief.

Bill Gates did not design Windows for a world that desired his operating system at the time. He created it at an age when the majority of people had no idea what an operating system was, but he was correct to believe that his system would become necessary and well-liked as times changed.

Steve Jobs went against the prevailing notion of what phones should be when he designed the first iPhone. He built a distinctive brand because he thought that consumers would appreciate his brand identification and distinctive touch and purchase his goods as a result.

Based on their respective knowledge and concepts, Jobs and Gates were both operating.

The Relationship Between Self-Belief and Confidence

People devote a lot of attention to developing their confidence, and for good reason. I all, who wouldn't want to have greater confidence? Being more confident makes you less fearful of failing, more open to trying new things, and more motivated to put in more effort when you put in the effort. It sounds amazing, doesn't it? Who wouldn't want everything like that?

I'm here to inform you that confidence is a trait that cannot be acquired! It's something you make, something you construct within, and it all begins with self-belief.

If you think of yourself as a hard worker or someone who can solve problems, you'll persevere through difficulties and do your best to find a solution. However, if you think you don't put in enough effort,

This applies to every aspect of life. Individuals who do not think they are beautiful sometimes have less dating prospects because they are not willing to put themselves out there. People become famous in social settings not because of their personality or interests, but rather because of their self-assurance and conviction that they are engaging individuals. People share their hobbies and ideas and become more sociable once they have this belief. More in-depth talks occur when people have confidence in their capacity to lead effective conversations. All of this strengthens the conviction even more because it has been demonstrated to be accurate. This pattern keeps happening and

CHAPTER 2:SELF BELIEF

fosters strong social confidence.

To what end does this lead? So, what would be your response to a silent, gloomy-looking stranger who makes no attempt to engage with you? Suppose, however, that you decide to take the risk and introduce yourself. The person you are speaking with reacts, but he or she does so in an extremely uncomfortable way and only provides brief, vague responses. How likely is it that you two will become friends if they don't provide you with any information, don't actually ask any questions, or don't delve deeper into the conversation? Not in the slightest, is it? This is the result of lacking self-belief and confidence.

The effects also extend beyond. The encounter has just not gone well for the one who lacks belief. They leave feeling uncertain and uncomfortable, relieved that the conversation is over,

When we look around, we frequently see that these spirals—whether positive or negative—create the individuals who are successful or unsuccessful. There are a ton of prosperous individuals in the world who received protection and nurturing for their self-belief as youngsters. Their personalities are shaped in a way that encourages an independent, daring lifestyle and provides them with the resources and coping techniques need to pursue this sort of career. They develop the habits of working hard, having confidence in themselves, taking calculated risks, and accepting mistakes from an early age. They could also adjust and grow from their errors. They eventually become successful adults as a result of this success and succeeding habit.

These people are less prone to take chances or risks since their first focus is their safety. They will tend to remain with what they already know is safe and secure. They have been protected in this manner and have lived this way up until now. Evolutionarily speaking, it's a reasonable decision. When it's not necessary to take a chance, why not? The issue is that these people are unable to distinguish between a risk that is justified, one that is calculated, and one that has the potential to truly change their lives. Anything might be fatal to a person who lacks self-belief in terms of their life or mental health.

The distinction between confidence and self-belief is the scope and impact of the former.

Usually, when we discuss self-belief, we're speaking more broadly. If you have a strong sense of self-worth, you'll probably be open to trying anything, even if it's a completely new ability or something you're not normally excellent at. Self-believing people don't require validation of their aptitude. They'll gladly attempt most things and have faith in their own abilities, or at least in their capacity to learn and grow.

Right now, I can assure you that confidence is worthless without self-belief. A person who lacks self-belief yet is confident in their abilities might be easily constrained. Recall that competence stems from performance in that domain; this is what validates their skills and provides them with confidence.

When faced with challenging questions, incorrect responses, and a great deal of learning, confidence begins to erode. The mathematician will now start to have some difficulty, and when that happens, they will start to have self-doubts. They lose confidence and eventually perform worse and worse. When considering this scenario, it is simple to understand why confidence on its alone is insufficient for sustained success. Your confidence restricts you to the skills and abilities you currently possess, as well as the degree of performance you can reach. Any increases after that must be modest and steady.

Contrast this with a self-assured mathematician who understands that all it takes is perseverance and hard effort to learn everything and achieve any degree.

Building Self-Belief

Most likely, you've heard of folks who are "driven." I don't mean driven about in a car; rather, I mean those individuals who just appear determined to succeed. Elon Musk and Michael Jordan are examples of individuals that will not give up until they succeed. Michael Jordan values it so highly that he published a book titled Driven From Within. Driving must be significant if one of the greatest athletes of all time thinks so highly of it.

Take another look at the title of his book. What motivates him? Well, we already know that it originates "from within." Would you like me to explain how he gets such amazing drive? His faith in himself provides the fuel.

How much he believes in himself is really evident. Putting that aside, though, it's obvious that he is speaking about everyone rather than just himself. MJ has acknowledged that everyone has limitations, but he also believes that everyone can accomplish in most things with enough effort, unlike most individuals who use limitations as an excuse for their unfavorable circumstances. The foundation of self-belief is knowing that you are capable of succeeding. Because most people have somewhat comparable potential and because others have achieved, you can also succeed.

Are you a future NBA star? It's quite improbable right now, but you could have been if you'd been motivated enough to practice continuously since you were able to walk. Without working nonstop throughout their youth, the Williams sisters would not be celebrities today. Had MJ not been a lifelong student of his craft throughout his childhood, he too would not have become a legend. These are life's realities. It is no accident that nearly all of the highest achievers in every industry have dedicated a great deal of time and effort to reaching their objectives.

Now that you have faith in your ability to accomplish, it's time to work hard. The second pillar of self-belief is this. You work hard and do the task efficiently. Too many individuals are preoccupied with continuing to be "busy" rather than paying attention to the most crucial task at hand. Be wise and take action instead than just studying and knowing.

This is the way of thinking of a man who, at the height of his talent, gave up a brilliant ten-year NBA career to try his hand at playing baseball in the Major League Baseball (MLB). In basketball, Jordan has admitted to missing countless shots, losing hundreds of games, and missing game-winning shots several times. He is still regarded as the best of all time, though. Why? Since failure is irrelevant.

Failure passes. It's an educational opportunity. It doesn't matter how many loses it takes to get there—what counts is whether you can win in the end. You will occasionally fail if you are genuinely pushing yourself and working hard. But that's alright. Everybody makes mistakes.

Accept the setback and look for lessons in it; failure makes a far greater teacher than triumph. Examine your findings and the process that led you to them. Is there anything you might have done better to increase your chances of success? Did you do actions that weren't required or that didn't matter? Consider failure as a necessary step on the road to success. By eliminating possibilities, you have discovered a different approach, which has brought you one step closer to the correct solution.

Recall that it is folly to do the same thing and expect different outcomes! Never do that!

After you've gained as much knowledge as you can from

each setback, incorporate it into your next strategy. Make adjustments and adjust to avoid failing.

The Importance of Self-Image

Alright, we've talked about desire, confidence, and self-belief. Let's now discuss one's own image. Self-image is the combination of your thoughts, feelings, and perceptions of who you are. Many individuals ignore this area, but if you want to develop particular abilities and habits or establish a certain lifestyle, it's crucial.

Recall how persons with poor self-esteem frequently act in ways that contribute to their unfavorable expectations? It turns out that self-image functions similarly. You are more prone to act in ways that reflect your poor self-perception, such as being inept, lazy, or useless. If you consider yourself to be a talented, hardworking individual, you are more inclined to act in this way.

This does not imply that you have to start out perfectly disciplined or productive. If that were the case, by the time we got to the point where you were an expert in this field, you would already be extremely focused and disciplined, so there wouldn't be much value in us talking about self-image. The wonderful thing about self-image is that it is something you can genuinely cultivate through tiny acts. For example, you can begin by creating and adhering to a basic routine for yourself if you want to see yourself as an active achiever, a problem solver who completes tasks and remains productive. Having a regular bedtime and wake-up time, as well as consistently preparing oneself for success in the morning by showering,

You'll notice a shift after merely a week of living this way.

Back in my college days, all I really did to establish solid habits was adjust my sleep pattern and begin implementing the 5-minute rule. Even if I was only going to sit in my dorm and work on my laptop all day, I would still make sure I smelt good and looked decent every morning. When I dozed out at my friends' house after a night out a few weeks later, I realized just how significant the consequences had been. I was miserable and disgusted when I got up since I was unable to get dressed properly—I didn't have any clean clothing, a toothbrush, or aftershave!

Over the following several weeks, I became more aware of my tendency to take the lead in group settings and to be more self-reliant in my work and learning. From then on, I began to occupy my free time with other useful pursuits and started the process of developing into the prosperous business coach and consultant that I am today. It's never easy to say exactly when someone succeeds, but I know that for me, it all started with my perception of myself.

This kind of self-image work gives you the power to select who you want to be. Depending on your goals, you may establish your own criteria and work your way up from there to develop your reputation. For me, it resulted in the creation of a "expected state," or way of life.

This kind of self-image is another technique to motivate yourself. Your perception of yourself as a dedicated worker who never gives up can only last if you consistently demonstrate it. The proof gradually strengthens the picture, which in turn gives you greater resolve, motivation, and the capacity to go deeper, all of which feed the image even more. It's a constructive cycle that you ought to use to advance.

3

Chapter 3: Self-Belief and Weakness

I collaborated with a group of Eastern European businesses a few years ago. Their diverse origins and comparable ages made for an intriguing group of individuals. The CEO had told me in advance that there were a few really good performers in the group and had enquired as to whether it would be possible to pinpoint these individuals' characteristics so that the rest of the group could concentrate on picking up their skills.

I've learned from psychology that humans often just have a few fundamental alternatives for handling most circumstances. I made an effort to discover theirs by posing targeted queries about their prior performances and strategies for success. I found that they would all talk about making constant effort.

Identifying Weaknesses

For some people, it might be difficult to admit they have a weakness since their ego is weak. Low self-belief leads to that, thus cultivating a good self-image and starting with your self-belief are always important. Most individuals still find it awkward to honestly evaluate and critically analyze oneself, but with time, it becomes less difficult. Finding your weaknesses involves more than simply modifying your company strategy or sales strategies; it also entails improving all aspects of your life, including your knowledge and abilities, behavior, and style of living.

The world's most successful people are able to see where they and their companies need to develop. When it comes to discipline, we must do this.

It's not uncommon for folks to battle with procrastination.

Many really successful celebrities still have difficulties with it. The important thing is to have control of it. Some individuals merely need to get more sleep, others need to make a plan and be more organized, while still others benefit from making

CHAPTER 3: SELF-BELIEF AND WEAKNESS

nutritional adjustments. Another strategy to develop a healthier and more productive mentality is stress management. I find that practicing mindfulness and meditation greatly helps in these areas.

Science has already shown that meditation causes changes in the body. It has been demonstrated that meditation increases attention and concentration while lowering stress levels and a number of ailments.

Returning to our theme of weakness, you must first recognize the problem and then devise a solution. Start with the largest issue and work your way down to smaller ones, and you'll soon realize how this may transform your life.

It also pertains to your character and interpersonal interactions.

It might be beneficial to reflect critically on your relationships in order to develop your own identity. This ability to create a character with the stats you like is nearly like being God in an RPG. You may project your image in whatever way you like, which makes it ideal for the professional world. Make up a character, then embody it.

NLP may not be unfamiliar to some of you. For Neuro-Linguistic Programming, it stands.

It's similar to changing the way you behave to enhance your weak points. You modify as needed based on the performance you want to achieve. It is possible to modify social skills in this way. Let's assume you want to get better at having conversations and you feel like you don't really go out there enough. Talking as much as you can is a great way to practice. Just start a discussion with someone, wherever you may be. Over time, with all of the extra experience, you'll become much more adept at holding interesting conversations.

You could discover how to improve when you try new things and come up with a cunning two-level plan. You'll be testing it in real life as well as comprehending what should work.

Changes in discipline are more closely associated with stepping outside of comfort zones and following a plan of action. You can push yourself beyond of your comfort zone to develop a natural inclination there. Work out a lot, take cold showers, and perform difficult exercises. You may step outside of your comfort zone in business and other spheres of your life with the aid of all of this. Developing and adhering to habits, even small ones like stretching at night, will make you more disciplined all around. Establishing routines such as these is crucial. However, there is one behavior that is significant at first and gets much more significant with time. What's that?

Self-Control

One component of everyday discipline that is crucial is self-control. You're going to tumble off fairly quickly without it. To paraphrase Jocko Willink, the "Task Unit Bruiser" leader of SEAL Team 3:

"Nobody wants to leave that comfort—that warm blanket and soft pillow—but if you want to get ahead of everyone else, you have to."

"American Sniper" Chris Kyle and other members of Task Unit Bruiser all experienced intense fighting in Iraq. Willink, a 20-year veteran of the SEALs, has always emphasized discipline as the secret to his success. The title of his second book is even "Discipline Equals Freedom."

Jocko promotes several easy methods that give you more control over your life.

Over time, self-control becomes increasingly crucial since some people tend to lose motivation as positive outcomes start

CHAPTER 3: SELF-BELIEF AND WEAKNESS

to show.

These positive outcomes make individuals overconfident and think they've already arrived. I have experienced this in the past as well.

I periodically dabbled in side companies throughout high school and university to supplement my income. These were straightforward local activities rather than large, spectacular constructions.

For the most part, I was successful. The problem is that I slacked off when I had enough money to get by, which led to each project finally dying a lingering death. If I had kept hungry, I could have accelerated and earned a lot more money, but my own success ultimately proved to be my undoing. I lacked the self-control to turn down temptation.

Furthermore, control goes beyond what you do. It also affects your feelings and thinking. Referring back to NLP, you can develop the kind of person you want to be if you can master your own thinking process. Regaining control over one's thoughts is related to mindfulness. In summary, mindfulness increases your awareness of your ideas as they arise and your ability to disassociate from them. In this manner, you are able to watch them and get rid of them if not needed. To achieve the desired mental state, combine this with deliberate positive thought generation. Despite how easy it seems, it's not since everyone has a lot of erratic, uncontrollable ideas.

You can react to circumstances more effectively when you have emotional control. David Goggins, an ultra-endurance athlete and former Navy SEAL, US Ranger, and paratrooper, comes to mind in this situation. This man is a real machine, and part of his strategy is to push himself outside his comfort zone all the time. Why? He is therefore familiar with the sensations of pain, agony, and tension as well as what it's like to be injured.

This man has transformed himself into someone who cannot be influenced emotionally—he won't let it—after leading an incredibly difficult life.

He has emotions just like everyone else, yet he has the ability to suppress those feelings, look past them, and act logically when necessary.

If you want to achieve in life, you must do this since mistakes will occasionally be made. Experiencing strong emotions won't assist when they do. You have the ability to select the best answers if you can learn to regulate your emotions. Additionally, you can resist giving in to emotional blackmail. Having emotional control makes it easier to overcome obstacles, deal with failures, and even just keep up a constant effort in general. It takes away the need for affirmation or positive reinforcement and enables you to function without them, like Navy SEALS like Willink and Goggins did.

4

Chapter 4: Mental Toughness

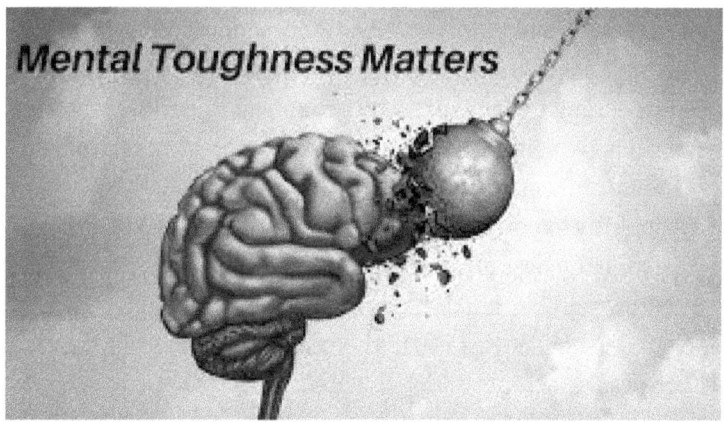

While drive and direction are wonderful qualities, they are insufficient on their own without the additional quality of mental toughness. One definition of mental toughness is the capacity to endure adversity.

These "bad circumstances" might be anything at all, such as an illness, inclement weather, or a challenging scenario overall.

It doesn't always have to be something horrible; sometimes, it might just be an abrupt and unanticipated shift. We all need and benefit much from mental toughness, especially when faced with hardship.

As we discussed when we studied Gates, Bannister, and four-minute miles in Chapter 1, the power of the mind is an incredible thing. Faith may motivate you to accomplish your goals,

My finest observation of this occurred at a training camp conducted by the military. A few weeks before to this session, the participants underwent fitness testing. The findings were shown on a clipboard for me to see, so I could tell who was the fittest and strongest. Furthermore, I understood that the physical demands of this camp would leave them all exhausted and that the main tests would be cerebral ones.

During an early practice, a few circuits and a fast run were used to exhaust everyone. The group was then instructed to perform bodyweight exercises together, matching rep for rep.

"I couldn't keep up with the rest; it was too much."

It's not my expertise; I'm just not as powerful as the others."

"Despite my best efforts, it proved to be too much for me."

See how self-centered these reasons are? Although they first appeared to have little faith in themselves, this was not the case. Toughness is lacking, and it's evident.

Toughness comes into play when things get rough. When uncertainty attempts to come in, it's like a nightclub bouncer. Being tough prevents comparisons and ideas of weakness by pushing it aside and suppressing it. This kind of powerful mind doesn't think about the task's completion or compare itself to others.

It is precisely this mentality that enables someone who is physically weaker to outwork someone who is stronger. The

CHAPTER 4: MENTAL TOUGHNESS

psychologically tough individual may do much more since they approach every activity, task, and every rep as a unique challenge. It was evident during our exams when I asked some of the less proficient students how they managed to perform so well. These were a few of the responses:

"I didn't think about anything other than the next rep."

"Unless I was unable to finish the exercise due to physical limitations, I had no intention of stopping." I was still going even if I performed several poor repetitions.

"There was still some in the tank; there's no need to stop until it's completely empty."

As you can see, these folks were only paying attention to what was right in front of them and to themselves. Some of them saw every rep as a test to see if they could complete it or not. It's common practice to break down difficult tasks like this in order to accomplish them. The process is called "chunking," and in Part Two, we'll examine it in further detail. It entails segmenting a lengthy or challenging work into manageable steps or chunks. This may be done with comprehensive programs, challenging activities, or simply one rep at a time or ten seconds at a time. All that's left to do is handle the little piece.

Why is this effective? Because you only see the outside when you compare yourself to other people. You are seeing someone do a workout, but you are not experiencing their agony, fatigue, or sense of impending quitting. People appear more stronger than they actually are from the outside (as long as they don't express any pain or concerns).

Compare this to your personal experience, where you are exhausted, in pain, and doubtful. Even while you know every rep hurts, you tend to forget it when you observe someone else. It is understandable why it is not a good idea to compare your results here. When you compare yourself to someone else, you are aware of your own suffering but are unaware of theirs.

Mental games and comparisons are eliminated when your attention is solely on the work at hand. There's no longer any need to judge people by their circumstances or feel as though you're having a worse time than they are. You put more emphasis on your athletic prowess than these judgments and sentimental ideas. Could you maintain the posture for an additional few seconds? Act at that time. You still had one rep left?

Take it out. Many people who use this approach will believe they can only perform one or two more repetitions, but they should really be able to perform ten more before their bodies start to fail physically.

Additionally, there is no pressure since you are not focused on the finish line or the enormous amount of work that has to be done. You're focusing just on the "chunk" that's in front of you, completely disregarding those. Take care of that part, that's all. Forget even about the conclusion. When everything is said and done, you will have either cleared every piece and finished the assignment or cleaned as many as you could and discovered your true limit—that is, your physical limit, not what your mind thinks the limit is. Don't give up if you still fail after doing this. Even if it's just for this one chance, you may relax knowing that you have reached a goal that most others never will.

Dealing With Doubters and Failures

To achieve at the greatest levels, you must possess extreme mental toughness. Since the greatest levels are the hardest, there will be problems and frequent change in the settings. At the highest levels, uncertainty in oneself is not the only thing that might cause issues; doubts in other individuals can also be problematic.

The parent-child dynamic is the best illustration of this. I have lost count of the number of times I have witnessed parents advise their children to set realistic objectives, telling them that pursuing a career in college and a regular job is more important than becoming a professional athlete, singer, or movie star. However, there are children who become professional sports, singers, and movie stars,

Taylor Swift is the ideal illustration of this. She had always wanted to be a famous pop artist, and her parents had supported her desire from the beginning. Her parents encouraged and supported her goal, which was the source of her motivation and self-belief. Through difficult times and early setbacks, they continued to encourage her, which helped her develop mental resilience. Swift heard several times in her early career that she wasn't talented enough to be a musician. In any case, she persisted in honing her trade and pushing herself. Currently, her net worth exceeds one billion dollars, making her one of the most recognizable and marketable individuals around. Nobody can dispute that she is all she had imagined.

How many more people who may be Taylor Swift are there now, doing 9 to 5 jobs because they were instructed at an early age to be realistic?

How many would-be celebrities never gave it their best because they believed others who thought they weren't good enough?

You may hear comments along the lines of "you're trying to do the impossible" or "you're not good enough" at some point in your life. It's acceptable to be intimidated by your lofty objectives since they will seem daunting to others. People are inclined to think you are incapable of reaching something if they think it is out of reach for them. It's critical to keep in mind that, ultimately, their viewpoint is meaningless.

If you do happen to run into someone with insider information, take use of their insights on how things operate, how to achieve your goals, and what it takes to advance. Take what you've learned from their experiences and apply it to further develop your skills. Ask for useful advise instead of opinions, and make sure you follow it through. The finest praise you can offer someone who is successful is to watch you make excellent use of their information, which they love to share.

The other thing that might make you fall behind is failure. As I previously mentioned, Taylor Swift experienced several setbacks and was told she wasn't good enough. Her response is the most effective one to employ when facing any setback:

She adjusted her strategy and continued honing her art until she at last received the desired acceptance. This manifested itself in album sales and a record deal. Unless you allow it to be, failure need not be fatal. Consider every setback as a teaching opportunity. Indeed, there are instances when it's advantageous to fail since each setback is an opportunity for growth and learning. You will get stronger and more accomplished after each setback if you apply this strategy to your own process.

You will inevitably get stronger and wiser with this method, and eventually you will be able to achieve your goals.

5

Chapter 5: Willpower

"A person's lack of will is what separates a successful person from others—not their lack of knowledge or strength." — Vince Lombardi

"Perseverance is based on willpower." — Napoleon Hill

"There is always a way if there is a will." - Anonymous

From the millions of quotations about willpower, these are only a handful. It has consistently been a major subject in self-improvement. Many prosperous individuals emphasize it as one of the most crucial elements of their success formula. What then is willpower? It's the capacity to restrain your own urges, to put it simply. Can you maintain a predetermined course of action when faced with unforeseen events? This is the nature of willpower. It's the ability to refuse food even when you're really hungry since it's not yet time for your scheduled meal. It's far simpler to just take a day off and relax than to get up and go to the gym when you're already exhausted.

Although willpower is undoubtedly already well-known to you, you might not be aware that it can be developed, just like any other muscle in the body. The prefrontal cortex, which makes reasoned decisions, is the area of the brain that controls willpower.

Willpower is comparable to physical muscle areas in that it may deteriorate and diminish if it isn't used. Bad habits might develop from a lack of self-control and discipline. Remember that this does not exclude you from sometimes taking time off. The secret is to include a few tiny, willpower-requiring behaviors into your daily routine and maintain them. It's completely fair to enjoy life in other areas if you can maintain a few minor willpower decisions, such as eating properly, exercising for limited periods of time each day, or setting aside time for wake-up calls. Just remember to maintain moderation! This implies that you cannot just go crazy every weekend and then expect to have strong control on vacation or on special occasions. Still,

Researchers have demonstrated that making decisions and suppressing urges are functions of the prefrontal cortex. This is the region in lab experiments that becomes active while making decisions and stays powerful and in control when subjects maintain their willpower. Other areas of the brain that are related to the desires being felt at the moment are activated by impulse reactions. When these regions become excessively active and the prefrontal cortex is fatigued and unable to keep up, bad judgments happen. This is the physiological process that takes place in your brain when you make an impulsive choice.

The good news is that research has also demonstrated that, similar to how it may be weakened by inactivity, this area can be strengthened by frequent use. Your prefrontal brain gets stronger as you make more deliberate decisions. One effective method to begin utilizing this knowledge is to incorporate minor decisions based on willpower into your everyday routine. Establish a consistent wake-up time that you will honor. One of the best ways to prevent impulsivity is to make a treat list the day before and stick to it.

When you are trying to get yourself motivated to go to the gym, it is easy to feel or think that you need a day off. It's simple to take you.

As I previously mentioned, you should maintain a few strong routines that help you create willpower when you take a break or go on vacation so you're still prepared to work when you get back to work. Similar to this, you may start with easy practices that will encourage the growth of your willpower muscle if you have little willpower to begin with and wish to build it. You may, for example, make yourself push through rigorous workouts, completely abstain from junk food, or make yourself take a cold shower each day. You should force yourself to accomplish something every single day that will improve your life and defy your present comfort-seeking tendencies.

Measuring Willpower

Let me tell you right away that it is impossible to gauge a

person's precise level of willpower. However, we are aware that each person has a finite quantity. There is a limited amount of willpower in each individual, but it can be increased or decreased based on how often you practice working on it. This is because the prefrontal cortex may be strengthened or diminished. Consider it like a willpower tank; each person has a distinct capacity. By following the correct procedures, you may adjust yours daily to a slightly larger or less amount. Every day need to begin with a full tank. Generalized stress, persistent lack of willpower, substance misuse, and even lack of motivation can all have an impact on this.

I once met a phenomenal athlete who competed on a global scale. This gentleman did an excellent job of keeping himself in check and performing at his best. However, I was working with him because, during the previous 12 months, there had been some irregularities in his discipline. Even for a typically well-behaved elite athlete, tournament results were not always as good as anticipated, and diet was not always consistent. I went over his calendars and diaries when we first started working together to see if there was anything I could use to explain what was going on. Everything appeared to be going according to plan; the timers had set their training intensities to peak, the recuperation appeared to be going well, and everything should have been alright.

We had to adopt a new strategy because the diaries were unable to provide an answer. What I did was accompany this athlete to his next competition and remain with him for a while. Not all the time, as I wouldn't want to divert his attention, but frequently enough to see that our athlete wasn't recuperating as effectively as feasible due to sleep issues brought on by the strange bed arrangement.

CHAPTER 5: WILLPOWER

We started discussing his sleeping arrangements when I learned that he had lately gone through a lot of stressful events, such as moving houses. His overall willpower had been undermined by all of this, and after looking over his journal and interviews more closely, we discovered that the sporadic lapses in exercise or nutrition may all be connected.

This demonstrates to you the significance of controlling your lifestyle, mind, and body in order to become a well-oiled machine. Anyone may be derailed by small things that weaken their resolve, just like an excellent athlete.

Being as healthy and well-rested as possible is ideal when it comes to achievement and personal growth. Let's return to the willpower meter now.

Research has indicated that throughout the course of the day, an individual's propensity to make poor and rash judgments increases. Because their willpower is worn down in the late hours of the day, they are more prone to act impulsively. This, in my opinion, relates to the reason that a lot of prosperous individuals wake up early every morning.

Consider this: they get started early and work with strong willpower levels. They'll be most productive and get the crucial stuff done early in the day. The day goes on, and the duties get easier and less demanding of willpower. This kind of "day design" is beneficial for developing discipline and success in all endeavors.

You need to make the greatest use of your willpower now that you are aware of its limitations. It's a good idea to start your day by tackling the most difficult things first. It also makes use of momentum, which is also very important. You see, if you make poor choices early in the day, it becomes more difficult to refocus since your prefrontal brain has already been challenged.

Negative momentum is created when you override it on small choices like skipping breakfast or getting out of bed.

Because you overrode your willpower, it is nearly nonexistent, which increases your likelihood of making poor judgments.

Imagine the individual who repeatedly ignores their alarm clock to avoid having to wake up at the crack of dawn. In addition, this individual is not dressing; instead, they are remaining in their pajamas. Let's say they have a mainly free day but also some work, cleaning, or even chores to complete. How probable is it that they will complete these duties in the end? If they succeed, are they inclined to go above and above, complete more tasks, or dedicate time to personal development?

No, since they will be limited to the absolute minimum by negative momentum.

On the other hand, you may put yourself in a stronger position to finish challenging chores if you begin the day with a few little momentum boosters (such changing your bed, having a shower, or putting out the garbage). greater belief, a stronger will, and greater discipline are produced by positive momentum. This helps you ease into the first significant activities and finish them before your willpower runs out, which is beneficial if you want to have a productive day. Imagine someone who, in contrast to our previous example, gets out of bed at the first sound of the alarm, gets ready, clothes nicely, and even has a pleasant scent. Now picture this individual having a somewhat free day with a few duties to complete as.

It's simple to see this individual working without interruption and finishing the task at hand, isn't it? Consider the converse. How likely do you think this vivacious person is to just sit down, ignore what they should be doing, and simply spend the rest of the day watching TV? This person always gets up and gets the early duties done no matter what.

Come on, you're probably going to ride that momentum a bit longer and get everything done, leaving you with a guilt-free evening to enjoy, if you woke up, dressed, cleaned your room, and made your bed all within an hour of waking up.

Habits and Routines

By enhancing the part of your brain responsible for logical decision-making, you may increase your overall willpower. In Part Two, we will go further into them. We'll now take a quick look at one method: meditation. Frequent meditation has been demonstrated to remodel the prefrontal cortex, enhancing both the area's capacity to influence your brain and its efficiency.

Lowering your levels of cortisol, the stress hormone, also makes you less stressed and increases your durability and efficiency. Elevated levels of stress deplete your reserves of energy and willpower, which is why meditation is beneficial in two ways. It increases prefrontal brain strength and decreases cortisol levels.

See my other books for further information about meditation.

We're going to concentrate on how to strengthen your willpower for the time being. Reducing its usage is the easiest solution. Many of you are undoubtedly wondering why I'm asking you not to utilize willpower when we've just been discussing how to use it to grow muscle and not let it go to waste.

No, that is not at all what I am saying. I'm trying to explain that you can live your life using the same moral choices—which need effort—but you may do it in a way that gradually requires less and less willpower. What am I referring to?

An nearly instinctive behavior is called a habit. Although it may be virtually any kind of behavior, once it becomes a habit, the conscious mind and decision-making process are typically not engaged throughout the job. Because you've done the same thing repeatedly until it becomes second nature, you don't need to make decisions as much. By employing certain strategies, such as a trigger to initiate the habit and a reward to conclude it, you can expedite this task. It doesn't take long to train a habit. Once the habit is effectively formed, executing the behavior doesn't require as much willpower.

It's important to remember that the willpower gauge functions somewhat differently than a typical gasoline gauge in this situation. We already know that it functions somewhat similarly to a muscle in that it gradually empties out over time if it is not used. Although good habits primarily function automatically, they do appear to sustain your high level of willpower—possibly by slightly increasing it. Conversely, if you intentionally choose a poor decision, your willpower appears to weaken. It all comes back to our previous discussion of momentum. Your prefrontal cortex—the muscle that controls your willpower—really values momentum.

Since momentum is what willpower prefers to operate with, if you make a poor decision,

6

Chapter 6: Mastermind Planning

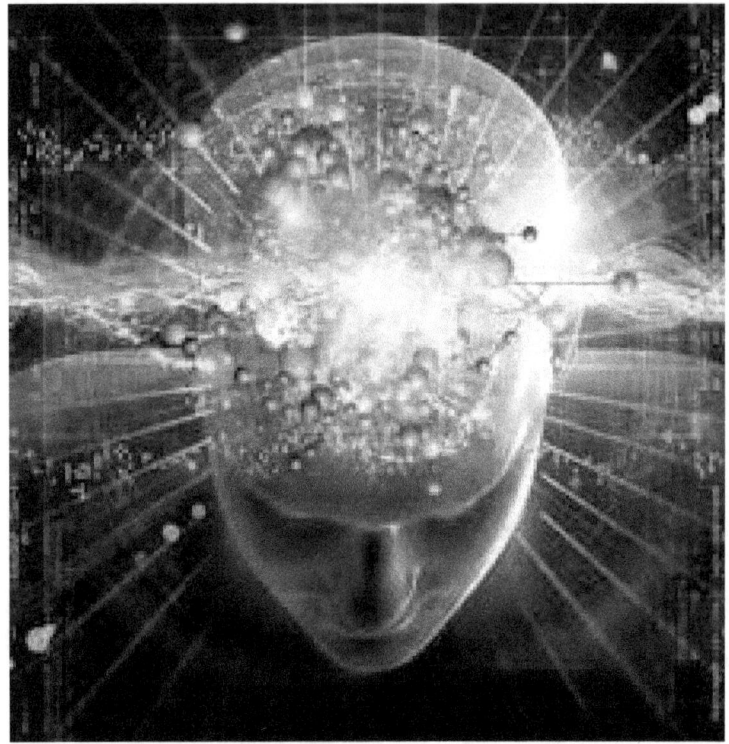

You know a lot about willpower now, don't you? Furthermore, you are aware of how to employ routines and habits to help you manage it a little bit better. It's time to develop this idea further now.

We've previously discussed developing the behaviors necessary to become the "you" you've always wanted to be. Developing one habit at a time—perhaps giving each one 30 days—was one of the topics we covered so you may gradually adjust to a new way of life. This works well for a certain kind of habit, but for others, it could be better to scale back or even extend over a longer period of time. Everything is dependent on how difficult the habit is going to be.

Habits – Small, Big and In Between

Being mostly unsupervised at initially was a major shock to my system when I first started university, as I recall. It was not like school, where teachers would always check to make sure you were in the correct location and finished all of your assignments. You are accountable for yourself while in college; no one will force you to work if you can't be bothered. They will accept your payment and not hold it against you if you flunk the course. You must put yourself in gear and get going if you're serious about moving forward and succeeding.

I had a terrible first year of school, just like a lot of freshman do. I had no trouble going out to parties.

After that, I felt as though I could separate the list into distinct categories. Many of my behaviors fit into the same category, requiring me to adopt them around every two weeks. However, there were a few that appeared really formidable. Eat healthily, that is?

What, constantly!? That is really challenging!

For me, these and a few other things fell into the "long" category since they appeared much more difficult than my typical routines. Another one in this part was "being fit," as I hadn't worked out in at least a few years and knew it wouldn't be a good idea to start at zero physical fitness.

"short" list: items in my life that ought to be simple to adjust.

For the majority of my habit changes, I continued to follow the "one-per-fortnight" guideline; but, for the "short" list, or the easy list, I made an effort to alter a habit every three days. Although you are free to choose a different timeline, it is not too difficult to make little adjustments every few days. If you stack them, they will stick with you since they are simpler tasks that require less willpower to do. These little routines accumulate concurrently with the modification of your primary habit.

The "long" modifications, or the challenging list, comes next. For this, you should divide it into manageable chunks, completing one every two weeks.

I added 30 minutes of exercise every two weeks by doing this. I was only working out for 30 minutes at beginning, which seemed manageable. But after two months, I was going to the gym four times a week for thirty minutes at a time and was in fairly good shape. I developed my habit over the course of four months, with three to four nearly-hourly sessions every week. I had lost a lot of weight at the end of my first year and was in the best shape of my life going into my second.

Building Your Future Self

It all boils down to effort and preparation when it comes to realizing your life goals. The outcome of those two things is everything else. One of the best quarterbacks in American football history, Peyton Manning, famously remarked, "I never left the field saying I could have done more to get ready and that gives me peace of mind."

This man had played in the NFL for eighteen years and was the best player there was from start to finish. He worked tirelessly and continued to have a significant influence even in his latter years. He was so good because of his work ethic, but notice this passage in the quote: "done more to get ready." It is discussing his preparation efforts. He was not just a diligent worker but also intelligent. He observed the tactics of the adversary, identified their patterns, and committed any vulnerabilities to memory. It was a shrewd move, and he coupled it with diligence to imprint in his mind the patterns of every opponent defense. This is how he used determination and astute effort to reach his full potential.

You have to take the same type of action in order to realize your ambitions.

All individuals has the capacity inside them. Conor McGregor, the MMA legend, is renowned for saying, "I'm not talented, I'm obsessed."

This quotation demonstrates the importance he places on his work ethic, self-belief, discipline, and thorough preparation. It demonstrates his conviction that everybody can develop into anything they choose and that natural skill isn't really important.

Once you realize that, you must reflect carefully and thoroughly on your life goals. These objectives are attainable, but they require the appropriate strategy and way of living. To put it plainly, you have to act like a billionaire if you want to be one. I don't mean wearing elegantly and splurging on clothing. I'm talking about working the "millionaire" hours—the early starts and late ends, the after-hours meetings to close transactions or develop your own firm. Make a list of the things this person does, how they live, and how they spend their time, and decide which behaviors will help you get where you need to go in life.

Now consider how your current way of living differs from your "target lifestyle." What should be altered? Create a list so you have it for future reference. It may be rather broad and all-encompassing at first, but you should gradually organize it into the "big," "small," and "medium" adjustments that must be done. You may now focus on implementing these adjustments and forming new routines one at a time. You start to mold yourself into the person you want to be in the future by forming these new routines and moving toward your ideal existence. Like with a sculptor, there is another thing to consider along the road.

"Take aim at the unnecessary." - Bruce Lee

Bruce Lee is a global legend.

You can't really benefit from bad habits because they just lead to disappointments and diminish your life. While it may be satisfying to indulge in more junk food or sleep late on the weekends, are you really accomplishing your objectives in the long run? Is it luring them a little bit further away instead?

You need to examine your poor behaviors and determine whether they are worth maintaining. Then, tackle them in the same manner as the positive habits, attempting to break each one individually. By doing this action, you can expedite the process of shaping your future self. It's a two-pronged strategy that combines creating positive habits with breaking negative ones.

Schedules

The use of schedules is another method for optimizing your willpower. This is not the same as a habit. A habit has to be consistent and occur on a regular basis. It's similar to having a set wake-up time or following a workout schedule. It functions well for recurring events, but life isn't always predictable.

The majority of individuals need to work harder in order to achieve in life. This is how they establish brands, start companies, and make a product to sell.

Doing any of that while working is difficult since you have other responsibilities to attend to. You might not want to try, even if you can get away with it.

I completely get how exhausting a job can be. There are hard, lengthy days. You will likely be exhausted by the end, and the thought of working harder might be disheartening. The task isn't easy with your own concepts either. You must choose the best course of action and what to do first. In addition, there are other aspects of life to manage, such as chores, socializing, and exercise. For anyone, dealing with all of this on top of their already-worn-out body from work would be scary. Your brain will want to start cutting things out because it doesn't want to deal with the effort and discomfort of getting things done, and your willpower tank is empty.

However, you may assist your brain here.

Never forget to allow yourself enough time for everything; otherwise, a timetable may backfire and increase your stress levels when you neglect to stick to it. Additionally, factors like trip durations, traffic, and other delays must be considered.

Now is the time to fill in the blanks with actions that will help you move closer to your objectives. That being said, you are free to take planned breaks when necessary and are not required to work nonstop. A crucial component of discipline is the practice of proper self-care. Similar to a machine, everything depends on you performing at your peak level. If you neglect your upkeep, a breakdown will eventually happen.

Chunking

You have the work at hand to focus on because of your timetable, so don't worry about what comes next. Simply perform the task at hand. This keeps your brain calm and is chunking in a different way. Maintaining a low cortisol level and remaining at ease also allows you to exert greater willpower. The key is to use your mind's power rather than allowing it to control you.

Divide a large, difficult task you have to do into smaller manageable parts. If necessary, you can further dissect these minor processes. Just work it out such that each action you need to perform may be converted into a task for your calendar. This is chunking as well.

You may make your larger goal more manageable by segmenting it into smaller segments. Writing an epic novel, for instance, takes a lot of labor, but writing a few pages is not too hard. But if you do it enough times, you'll have a book. When you combine that with a few rounds of planning and editing, you have a respectable book. After that, it basically comes down to studying, honing your technique, and making adjustments. In the end, though, you've succeeded in achieving a difficult objective by breaking it down into manageable pieces.

This is an additional method of overcoming the fear that comes with large projects. You now understand how to utilize chunking to complete large tasks and manage your time effectively.

Here's where chunking may be a useful trick of the mind. Remember that this requires confidence and practice. Practice and attempt it as often as possible ahead if you want to be able to pull it off when it counts. I apply this to my personal exercise regimen. It has also been mentioned by special forces operatives as one of their strategies for surviving the demanding selection process. It's the capacity to acknowledge that you will experience some discomfort and know that it will pass quickly. Let's say you have one minute to start. Do a second one after that.

However, it's not about taking things one minute at a time; rather,

But when I get there, I know I can go a little bit further, so I aim for 8 kilometers and stop there. I struggle towards the finish, but when I hit the mark, it gives me that extra little push. Now, one more kilometer feels awful. But five hundred meters? Let's carry that out. then the subsequent 300 meters.

Next, 200 more to reach 9 kilometers. Now that I'm almost

done, how can I not try for just a little bit more?

Sometimes the fate of a soldier in the special forces remains unknown. Occasionally, they are being sought for or have already been apprehended. It's difficult to be optimistic in these circumstances because, if you can't, you might not survive.

7

Chapter 7: Intelligence Versus Emotion

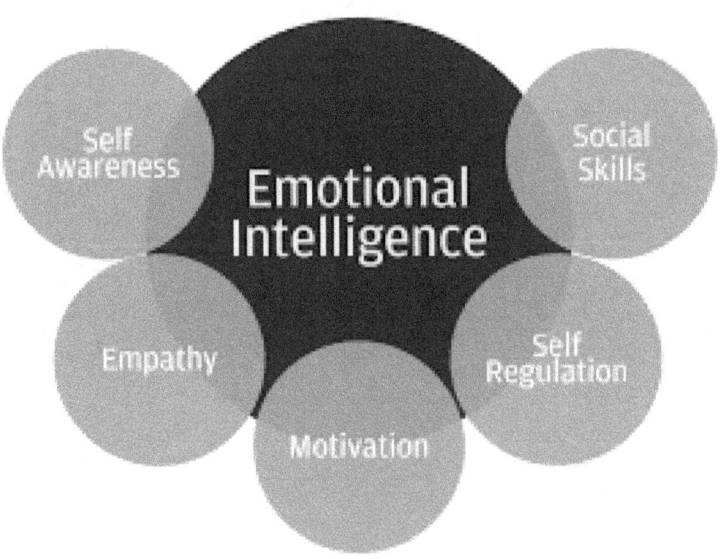

CHAPTER 7: INTELLIGENCE VERSUS EMOTION

You have an objective with the design of your master plan. Through sensible action and step-by-step breakdown, you may start along the path to achieving your objective. In the last chapter, we discussed personal development, making progress on your path, forming healthy habits, and breaking negative ones. You must be conscious of your progress, though, to ensure that everything is operating as it should.

Self-Analysis

They are working. It is in this domain that you must apply your intellect instead of your feelings. Feelings are called emotions. I'm the type of guy that holds myself to a very high standard. I often feel like I'm not accomplishing enough because of my feelings. Regretfully, this implies that there are moments when I truly struggle to finish my schedule and end up overcommitting myself to work. This negatively impacts my emotional state since I begin to feel anxious and depressed about slipping behind. Actually, I work at a rate that is generally higher than necessary; it's simply that my brain is trained to always feel like I should be doing more.

You must to constantly assess your performance honestly in all facets of your life. Are you creating sensible timetables that aren't either simple or excessively complex? Are you following them? Have you been following your strategy and developing positive behaviors as instructed? Have you been discarding the undesirables? Or have you occasionally acted a little carelessly, maybe making a few mistakes?

Keep in mind that mistakes are made by everyone. There's more to changing your life and your thoughts than just flipping a switch. It requires persistence and time. It's acceptable to make mistakes or to occasionally slack up on your standards.

Make the necessary changes to your approach or to hone a

few habits! A sincere and methodical approach is necessary to fully utilize your new mindset. Everyone makes errors and occasionally slacks off. That's how life works and how we develop as a result. It is important that you take a seat, go over your notes, timetables, and other plans, and then honestly assess where you are at. If you want to achieve, being honest with yourself is crucial!

You can also benefit from using analysis such as this one. It will highlight your strengths and the aspects you find most compelling.

How Emotions Affect Performance

Anyone who needs to perform professionally in a high-stress setting will tell you that emotional regulation is essential. Emotion may have a significant impact on athletes, warriors, and business people worldwide. These are the occupations where the consequences are easiest to observe. A player who performs poorly is more likely to lose their cool than one who does well. This is a result of their irritation at being ignored or unable to function.

Mike Tyson was completely destroying the professional boxing scene in the 1980s and 1990s. Tyson had an incredible run from 1985 to 1996, losing just once. Aside from a shocking defeat to Buster Douglas,

Tyson was stopped by Holyfield in the clinch of their first bout. He overstepped the bounds and employed some dubious strategies to subdue Tyson and win. He made the identical opening statement in the rematch. In a swift and heated moment, Tyson bit off a portion of Holyfield's ear in response. He was disqualified and barred from boxing as a result.

Oprah would interview Tyson years later and inquire about what transpired.

CHAPTER 7: INTELLIGENCE VERSUS EMOTION

Mike responds as follows: "I was upset because he was butting me. In the initial struggle, he sliced my skull and then did it again. I was enraged and furious. Though it's hardly a justification for what transpired,

One fighting sport is boxing. Both males are attempting to strike out and injure one another. Here, one of the all-time greats expresses his rage and frustration at being up against a superior opponent. He lost control of his emotions, which resulted in a humiliating occurrence and a significant setback to his career.

Instances such as this occur in sports worldwide. Examples of emotion getting the better of people include Zinedane Zidane hitting someone in the head, Novak Djokovic smashing rackets, and the Pacers and Pistons fighting on the floor.

There are elite athletes involved in each of those scenarios. These individuals are aware of the sensible strategy for succeeding in their athletics. They are driven and disciplined.

When it comes to performance, emotions do have a place. I already discussed Mike Tyson's lone setback during his initial 11 years of competition. In 1990, when Tyson was viewed as unbeatable and Buster Douglas as more of a gatekeeper than a contender for a title, it happened against Douglas. Tyson was expected to use the fight as a tune-up, winning handily before moving on to a high-profile match.

This was, however, Douglas's greatest battle to yet. He was exercising hard every day, giving it everything he had in an effort to please his mother. Douglas' mother sadly died away a few weeks prior to the bout,

Conversely, a lot of athletes succeed because they are driven by emotion. Many successful people have overcome adversity to reach success. Lebron James, Ray Lewis, and Floyd Mayweather

Jr. are a few instances of rags to riches tales. These folks used their difficult upbringing and unfavorable feelings into fuel. It gave them the drive to excel in their industry and maintain their position at the top. Their ability to control their emotions led to their achievement.

After his mother passed away, Buster Douglas took the same action. He used it to his advantage over the final few weeks of training camp. Then, he continued to think about it while fighting, waging his own battle and not backing down from Tyson's blows. For the most part,

Add to this the fact that Tyson was being affected by emotion. He thought this would be another simple victory, so he exuded an excessive amount of confidence and ease. After experiencing such great success in the previous several years, Tyson had relaxed throughout his training and was fighting almost without a plan.

He kept loading up in an attempt to get the one huge shot that would cap off the evening. When it appeared like Douglas was in trouble, he maintained his composure, maintained his distance, and dug a little bit twice. Even though he was knocked down in the ninth round, he was only just able to stay in the fight and win the count.

"Due to my mother."

It's the ideal illustration of how emotion can be controlled and used to improve performance.

You can now see that feelings may have both positive and negative impacts. Any emotion may be channeled, both constructively and adversely, by anger, and it doesn't even matter what that feeling is at the moment. The same is true of frustration and life's challenges. For melancholy, grief, and despair, this is true. Every emotion has an effect on our thoughts and actions.

It is possible for two persons with very similar backgrounds to have quite different outcomes depending on how they respond to various circumstances. A person might become pessimistic and spiral into a vicious cycle as a result of unfortunate occurrences.

The Evolution of the Human Brain

The majority of living things are brain-based. Some people are born without a brain because they are not in need of one. One example of a living being without a brain is a sea sponge. For millions of years, these sponges have been suspended on the ocean floor, collecting food particles and other nutrients from the surrounding water. They never have to make decisions, are aware of their environment, require sensory organs, or have the capacity to move; the filtering happens automatically.

Because it doesn't make their ability to operate or live any better than it currently is, this explains why they function so well without a brain. For such a species,

How do you find all of this relevant? All or most living things shared an ancestor billions of years ago, somewhere along the evolutionary timeline. If you go back far enough, you will likely discover a primitive creature that was able to obtain food and/or energy sources and procreate. It would have started off without a brain and could only carry out basic functions in order to survive and procreate.

This creature would have undergone mutations and developed throughout time. It would have divided into several distinct lines, each developing in a unique way. The sea sponge story was one of these old tales.

They are long-lived and do not require evolution, leading a basic and uninteresting life. Some lines become increasingly intricate.

Many of the evolutions from this organism would have resulted in larger, more complex species, such as the animals that live in the seas and on Earth today. These would have been the first animals to have sensory organs, a brain, and the ability to move about.

The majority of our ancestry may be found in the water, which is where life on Earth first emerged. The water would have been home to a variety of species back then, each with their own unique and amazing patterns.

Let's take the common, old fish as an example of a mobile organism. This animal would have to precisely navigate the water by swimming through it. In this habitat, it would have to be able to hunt or else acquire food, and it would have to consume something in order to get nutrients.

Even if this creature's brain is involved in so much more, a lot of it still needs to happen automatically. This is a result of the animal brain's lack of consciousness compared to the human brain. The brains of the majority of animals are programmed to make particular choices in response to their environment.

Ladybird beetles, sometimes known as ladybugs, are an excellent illustration of this.

If you stumble into one of these insects, it's pretty easy to catch and quite harmless. Although they have wings, they don't utilize them unless necessary. The ladybug will often wander around in peace and investigate if there isn't any food or danger around.

If you place one of these bugs on a stick, it will follow the trail to the finish, realize it has finished, and then turn back. The procedure will then be repeated.

To allow the insect to perceive a path off the stick when it first rotates, you must have your hand or anything else at the end of the stick. It will start the trip and stop processing any more data, such as the fact that the trail has vanished. It does not realize this until it reaches the conclusion. It searches for a different path at that point and moves in that direction. This method allows you to maintain an insect walking on the same stick for an extended period of time without it remembering anything. It operates just on what is available, not on memory.

It follows that the human brain is superior. Alright, to a certain extent. The basic animal brains that we had before developed into our sophisticated human brains were hardwired for survival. The sole concern of an animal's brain is survival, hence it will only respond in predictable ways. The human brain is primarily concerned with comprehending, adapting, and making the most of a given circumstance. At some point in our evolutionary past, humans started to transition between the two...

The Animal Brain Versus the Human Brain

The psychological effects of an animal brain's development can be rather detrimental to modern people. It appears that humans did not simply flip between the two types of brains. The human brain is the most amazing and sophisticated organ on the planet. Because we still don't fully understand how the brain functions as a whole, brain injuries may be extremely dangerous and difficult to cure, and brain surgery is extremely delicate. Literally, decoding the brain is more difficult than coding a supercomputer.

We do know that the brain is different from the brains of other animals and that it has gradually changed over millions of years. The basal ganglia region, which is central to our brains, has been compared to the brains of reptiles by several neuroscientists. Since this region of the brain is the deepest, it seems sense that it is the oldest. Animals that primarily rely on instinct may be seen in reptiles and birds, whose brains resemble this region. These creatures will look for sources of heat, food, and cover. They don't have many familial ties and a relatively simple social structure. They have an innate need to live, eat, and procreate.

More developed systems such as the hypothalamus and the amygdalae are located outside of the basal ganglia. These are the parts of the brain that enable us to form memories, according to research. They are also in charge of our hormone systems and emotions. The neuroscientist Paul MacLean coined the phrase "limb of the limbic system," which may be used to characterize these brain areas. According to his theory, this area of the brain evolved as our ancestors moved away from reptile lifestyles and toward a more mammalian one.

These creatures would have been capable of remembering the past and experiencing fundamental emotions. They would then be able to recall family members and be safe thanks to this fundamental level of memory. These animals may have hormone imbalances and feelings, and they may have preferences for particular meals, people, or hiding places. For this species, hard-wired reflexes are no longer the norm. It is still capable of making judgments based on survival instincts, which are influenced by memories. But as the system has evolved and there are now family groupings, for instance, this animal may also make emotional decisions.

A family group will frequently stick together and take care of one another, with the stronger members looking out for the weaker ones. Around this stage, parenting really starts to show, with adult animals caring for and protecting their young. Strong individuals used to go it alone in order to increase their personal chances of living, but these days they would stick together in order to increase the likelihood that the family's genetic makeup will survive. The transition from instinctive behavior to conscious thought, reasoning, and decision-making is well advanced.

At last, the neocortex—the most developed brain region—was developed.

Only higher animals have this region of the brain, which gives humans the capacity for language and information perception.

The human brain has evolved to this point, enabling us to function as the sentient beings that we are, although other brain regions still remain. These more archaic regions continue to play a significant role in our daily lives and have a lasting impact on us since, after all, they have survived for thousands of years and successfully maintained our genetic lineage.

These brain regions still function in a very primitive manner.

They nevertheless have a strong innate tendency to shun discomfort, suffering, and risk. The issue is that in today's world, success occasionally requires overcoming discomfort, danger, or agony. Everyone would succeed if there was no danger or suffering involved, isn't that right?

Understanding the Instinctual Brain

Your brain is programmed by evolution to steer clear of unpleasant feelings and situations. It acts in this way in an effort to maintain your happiness, health, and survival as the host animal. Your life will be better the happy you are.

Regretfully, the idea of future planning is beyond the animal brain's comprehension. It comprehends just the present moment.

Your human brain can comprehend at the deepest levels that short-term sacrifices of pleasure can have long-term benefits.

You may reap more rewards down the road by putting in more labor, effort, and discipline now that will cause some discomfort. This is something that your human brain is aware of and may arrange for you to follow. If you stick to the plan,

This strategy is beyond the animal brain's comprehension. It can only comprehend what is directly in front of it, which in this situation would be labor. It views labor as a disagreeable endeavor with no quick rewards because it provides no resources for you to reproduce with or nourishment. The animal brain views labor as a pointless endeavor that simply causes pain and drains your vitality. It is far preferable to continue lounging and relaxing until you have to perform a more important task.

Overcoming and outsmarting the animal brain is a major component of mental discipline. You must take conscious control of your life and cease living according to your instincts in favor of following the blueprint of your human brain.

You might start to conquer these sentiments by realizing why they arise. One major one is procrastination, as so many individuals wait until the very last minute to do any job. Why? In the event that it is subpar, they already have an explanation. In this instance, your animal brain is defending you emotionally and psychologically rather than just physically. The natural brain will steer clear of any unpleasant stimuli, whether they be perceived mental threats or actual physical ones. It will help you stay out of any awkward or challenging circumstances. It will do every effort to maintain your safety and security, free from any form of intimidation or confrontation.

The issue with this is that success demands great effort, which inherently forces you to step outside of your comfort zone! Growth comes from pushing yourself beyond your comfort zone!

You need to be extremely aware of what you are doing and

CHAPTER 7: INTELLIGENCE VERSUS EMOTION

why in order to break free from your ingrained routines. Accept the sensation while also being aware of its motivations, rather than fighting against what your instincts are telling you to do. Give it permission to exist and use a thoughtful approach to concentrate on the small discomfort of the task at hand and the significant reward when it succeeds. By doing this, your instincts will become more in sync with your intellect, enabling you to lead a more fruitful life.

The strength of the unfavorable emotions your instincts produce can be reduced by practicing mindfulness and relaxation practices. Being aware of these emotions and learning to relax yourself lessens their influence and enables you to be more present. You may fully comprehend and accept that nothing terrible will ever happen to you if you are present in the moment. Working a little isn't as bad as your gut may tell you, and you may build good momentum and drive by concentrating on the reward at the end and your motivations.

Your genuine route to happiness and prosperity is to live according to your higher brain's plan; your instincts should be telling you this, but they are unaware of it. The times have swiftly evolved,

I once questioned a professor at my institution about how he managed to finish his studies ten years ahead of schedule before starting his career. Wasn't he exhausted and bored after all the studying, tests, and dissertations? Was obtaining many PhDs worth it? For him, it was. For him, each year and each semester represented an additional phase in his grand scheme. All of this was pointing him in the direction of his goal: being the most in-demand expert in his nation for his specific field of expertise. He was aware that he might live the life he desired by being that. Day in and day out, his employment could be centered around his interest. He would receive more than enough money to live the life of his desires and be comfortable.

For him, this desire was worth ten years of hard effort, grinding away at his skill, and unpleasant learning. He overcame his instinctual brain at a young age, allowing his higher thinking brain to mold the life he desired. He is now content with his life, as he should be, and he keeps teaching the next generation about psychology and human nature.

You now know why it might be challenging to maintain discipline even when you know it's the right course of action for you. Knowing why this occurs can help you start fighting the ideas and emotions that could make you let up. Remind yourself of the long-term suffering and expenses associated with slackness and goal failure.

8

Chapter 8:Controlling the Mind

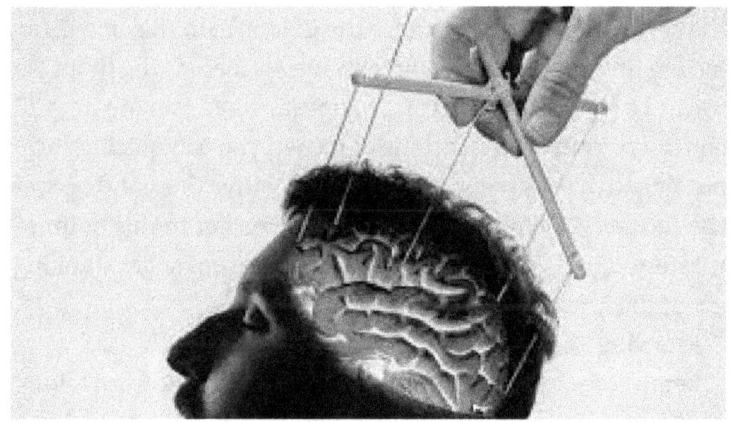

Control is the type of ability that everyone aspires to possess. Controlling people's thoughts and behaviors is essentially the same as controlling their brains. Since people act on their thoughts, they must first consider things out before acting on it. People can behave relatively impulsively or unconsciously, of course, but these choices are made either out of habit or as automatic reactions to prior experiences; in other words, your brain has already made up its mind about the optimal course of action without your conscious awareness.

There is no unique tool or method that can give you mental influence over other individuals. Possessing mental control is a kind of superpower in and of itself. You may already believe that you are in charge of your own thoughts, but if that were the case, you wouldn't require the guidance in this book. No, having the ability to block out extraneous ideas is the first step toward actual mind control. It appears when you are in total control of your mental attention, when you can quickly swap out negative or disruptive ideas for positive ones and ignore the former. Discipline gets easy once you get to this point of mastery. This is due to the fact that you are no longer thinking about the immediate discomfort,

Knowing Yourself

Being conscious of your ideas is the first step toward taking control of your mind and your thoughts. There is an old Greek proverb with unclear roots that begins, "Know thyself."

The origin of this proverb, which dates back many decades, is unknown, as is its actual age. This proverb is at least 2400 years old, as it was engraved at the Apollo Temple at Delphi, which was thought to have been built by the fourth century B.C. at the latest. Many individuals misinterpret this quote's original meaning or undervalue its significance.

CHAPTER 8: CONTROLLING THE MIND

"Aware of yourself? "Of course I know myself!" is the initial thought that so many individuals have when they read this phrase. understanding oneself has come to be valued more than understanding your adversaries or competitors throughout time. Sun Tzu believed that knowing your adversaries and oneself was crucial. Sun Tzu was a tactical genius who understood everything there was to know about fighting and battle. Knowing as much as he could about his adversaries' behaviors, attitudes, beliefs, loves, fears, and any other information that might help him understand them better was crucial to him. The only thing that could give him the advantage in combat was total understanding.

What he also understood was that he had to know himself. He was aware of his own inclinations and tendencies and examined them objectively, without of bias or emotion. He would look within and acknowledge his own shortcomings. He would discover his own strengths as well, and since he was aware of both of them, he could direct the conflict in ways that would benefit him more than his adversaries.

Sun Tzu understood that it's sometimes best to avoid taking advantage of your opponents' vulnerabilities due to your own. In other situations, you might be able to assault your opponent while he is at his weakest. It required more than just understanding the difference between strong and weak things; rather,

Beyond that, honesty is another aspect of understanding oneself. You should be aware of and resigned to the fact if you are easily flustered when faced with difficulties. You can find yourself in danger if you ignore it.

I was brought out on a team-building activity with several of my coworkers a long time ago. There are many similarities between the economic sector and the military and combat. One excellent illustration of this is the fact that Sun Tzu is still seen as having a significant impact on the contemporary corporate world. We were rehearsing this in full at the team-building activity, which had a military theme and was supervised by former military people.

Effective collaboration was essential to completing this objective. It was more crucial to get to know the team and divide tasks well in order to optimize performance than it was to focus on teamwork. Before the assignment started, we were unaware of all of this. What then did we do?

We obviously made an effort to maintain equality since that is the message that contemporary society has given us. Equality and fairness are being heavily pushed in the times we live in. It is a common belief that everyone is capable of doing whatever that another person can.

Naturally, this is true at a basic level as well; everyone has a same amount of potential to begin with. If the proper steps are followed, I think practically every young child can be trained and taught to excel in any subject. What I don't think any adult can do, in my opinion, is become another adult. We are all molded by our experiences and acquire unique characteristics and skills throughout our lives. A youngster is like a clean slate; most of them have enormous potential, even though they could have somewhat varied abilities. An adult no longer have the beneficial capacity to take in knowledge and learn quickly since they have already started to realize their limitations.

By expanding on the work of earlier specialists, contemporary scientists are able to advance society and make significant advancements. For instance, we have the best engineers in the world working on creating the next wave of technology, and we make the most of them by giving them all the resources and tools they require. In order for them to collaborate and expand on the expertise of their predecessors, we strive to assemble the greatest teams possible around them. However, we don't count on their making contributions to other facets of our society. Why, after all, would we?

If we requested the engineer to participate in fundamental building as well, can you image the waste of skill that would result? The engineers' time and energy would be squandered on a simple task that anybody could perform, yet no one is qualified to take their place in their true position.

This demonstrates how society may use its resources effectively to get the greatest results. Humans are not all the same or equal, as this illustrates. Every person is unique, and this is something to be honored. A person's expertise should never make them feel superior to others; even the most basic home builder is an important part of our society and should be respected for their abilities.

Let's return to our team-building task now. We had an issue here because we believed in equality so strongly. Instead of concentrating on how to do the task at hand, there was a lot of "fairness for the sake of being fair" since none of us wanted to admit to one another that we weren't excellent at anything.

We made sure that everyone was on watch duty at all times by rotating our lookouts. In order to minimize the amount of running back and forth that one person had to do, we also rotated our lead scout and evenly split up the duty of carrying the equipment. We would switch the carriers around every five minutes to maintain equality.

"Why were these small women carrying the same amount of gear as the large, 6'4" tanks? In order for you all to travel more quickly, why didn't you let the larger guys carry more?

Why did you choose to rotate your big guys in as scouts as well? They are easily noticeable as they approach the horizon, thus it is a waste of energy for them to try to move quickly and cover ground.

"Are you not aware that when you switch the lookout, a new lookout arrives who has no idea if the surroundings have altered or not?

They had never looked at the surroundings and landscape before.

"Why was there always so much debate and so many opinions whenever a choice needed to be made?

All of the points were well-made, and as they were brought up, they all appeared to make perfect sense. Naturally, we ought to have just handed the larger guys the most of the gear since they could handle it without becoming tired. They would have been able to move the equipment and be in excellent form overall, unlike a few of our smaller members who had been tired from having to lift big objects. If they needed a break later on, we could have switched for a short period.

Conversely, our larger men felt that leading scout required them to dash back and forth while attempting to locate paths and convey information, which was quite taxing.

The same held true for our leadership: it was preferable to let people who were most qualified for the position handle it. A stronger chain of command would have made it possible for each member to focus on their strengths, enabling the team to complete the objective more quickly and safely.

I've always understood how important it is to be aware of your talents and shortcomings ever since that day. You need to be really sincere with both other people and yourself. Prior to this exercise, I would always give any task my all. I no longer hesitate to turn down projects that might be a better fit for someone else. To some, this may seem choosy,

Determine your talents and weaknesses and work toward them if you want to advance in your own life. I used to struggle with procrastination. When you have the room to get away with it, it's quite simple to procrastinate and perform the bare minimum. I started to recognize this weakness—my propensity to back down when I had enough time or space to get away with it. My ability to perform well under pressure and my high morning productivity are two of my key qualities. I started scheduling my work so that it was primarily done in the mornings in order to take advantage of this.

I also had to come to terms with the fact that I would not be able to finish tasks before the deadline. For me, it just wasn't effective. Since the deadline itself served as my inspiration and motivation for work, I could work twice as long and yet produce the same results. Here, I came up with a solution that, although it worked for me, might not be that pleasant for other people.

Knowing oneself is crucial, once more. I knew that the stress would not break me; on the contrary,

Some individuals might find it difficult to follow the timetable because mine isn't very flexible. It all boils down to understanding who you are and how you operate. This timetable works perfectly for me.

It is convenient to be able to glance at it and have it direct me. Though I don't schedule end-to-end, I do allow myself some wiggle room in case I need it. I want to avoid having too much free time.

A to-do list that can be crossed off in any order may be preferred by certain people over a rigid, structured plan, while others may prefer something more ambiguous and flexible. It all boils down to self-awareness. What will suit your needs?

Mental Awareness

We discussed mind control at the beginning of this chapter and how you may train yourself and take charge of your life by learning to manage your own thoughts. You achieve this by becoming conscious of and in charge of your thoughts.

Our thoughts are the foundation of everything. These ideas have enormous influence since they shape our words, deeds, and sense of self. Recall your self-worth and the significance of having a positive self-image. This relates to what you were thinking.

There are many different types of individuals in the world, and they all interpret and absorb life differently. People think in various ways when it comes to thinking. Some folks are genuinely simply thinking about something.

The important thing to remember is that everyone has certain commonalities, regardless of how your ideas arise. Among these is the way our minds may become "intrusive." Any idea that arises without your conscious choice to consider it is considered invasive. Though everyone has these ideas occasionally, some people may experience them more frequently and intensely than others.

Most people begin to oppose the ideas or try to divert their attention by focusing on something else in an attempt to conquer these. This is a bad decision because the more resistance you offer the notion, the more force it gains. Since the goal of meditation is to become aware of everything around us, it might be a terrific approach to learn about this process.

Meditation helps you to be present in the moment and to notice the sounds around you, the temperature of the surrounding air, the feel of the chair, and the smells. When we meditate, we are taught not to name or label anything because doing so will pull us out of the present moment. We are also taught not to try to focus more intently on anything while we are meditating. It will bring your attention to something you have mentally defined and are expecting. Rather, simply relish the moment without any presumptions or anticipations.

If you are able to accomplish this with the noises and scents in your environment,

You are aware that you may decrease the influence of your instincts on you by understanding why they are occurring. This also applies to the way you think. They won't be able to control you if you can recognize them and watch them without being entangled or attracted to them. That's precisely what meditation teaches you to do—it teaches you to observe and let go of your ideas without becoming emotionally invested in them. Again, to learn more about how to accomplish this, I strongly recommend that you look into one of our guides on mindfulness or meditation.

The primary goal of meditation when you initially start out is just being aware of your thoughts. Novices will become disoriented in the idea,

As you get better at letting go of thoughts, you'll eventually reach a point where they just pass through your head without any connection, which will enable you to accept them and let them go before they have a chance to stick. At this point, you are not experiencing your ideas from within; rather, you are just witnessing them. Your awareness and vital force are now distinct from your mental process. Like every other organ in the body, the brain is an organ that is fueled by and serves you; it is not YOU.

By keeping an eye on your ideas, you may have a better

understanding of their origins and reasons for occurring. You will comprehend the rationale.

You'll uncover some crucial insights when the rationale for your ideas starts to clear out. Your evolutionary hard-wiring will be able to tell you what it is that it is striving to avoid. You'll be able to distinguish between a fear of failure and a fear of danger or exposure. You will be able to discern whether there are any old incidents that continue to resurface and impact you.

You'll be able to tell if your thoughts are driven by underlying dread or worry.

Not every response is unfavorable, though. Knowing why your thoughts happen and what you actually want might help you identify what brings you comfort and a sense of well-being. You are capable of determining how to effectively inspire yourself and your goals.

It involves realizing the consequences of procrastinating and lack of discipline, as well as how these behaviors will lead to long-term suffering in your life.

Although it's not magic, if you get the hang of it, it will seem that way.

Knowing yourself allows you to live a peaceful existence where everything has a purpose and an aim, and you always fully understand why things are the way they are.

You are far more likely to stick to your discipline and continue on the path to success when you know why you're doing what you're doing and have trust in the outcome.

Furthermore, you'll notice a gradual decrease in intrusive thoughts.

Your ability to focus will increase and your thoughts will wander less. Regular meditation also has a host of other beneficial impacts, such boosted immunity and less stress (as seen by decreased cortisol levels in the body). Recall what we mentioned about how ideas become words and deeds? You will have complete control over your thoughts at this point, able to get rid of any invasive or unpleasant ones. That makes it possible for you to live a negative-free life, which increases the likelihood that you will speak and behave in a good manner.

This is where positive momentum begins—in your thinking. If you persevere through it every day, you'll see that your discipline increases.

9

Chapter 9: Emotions, Fear, and Setbacks

Thoughts are a challenging domain to manage, the optimal approach has been discussed previously. If the techniques in this guide are applied as directed, anybody may take control of their own thoughts since they are effective for everyone. From here, everyone may mold their mental state and design the life they choose.

Imagine that at this point in your journey, you've made

enough progress to have control over your thoughts and are starting to experience success in all aspect of your life. Unexpectedly, a problem affecting your career and place of employment arises. You're suddenly under a great deal of stress, yet now more than ever,

Amidst all of this, you've had a negative event in your personal life. It may be something genuinely awful, like a loved one being gravely sick or suffering severe injuries. You're under even greater strain, and to make things worse, your family consumes all of your thoughts rather than the tasks at work.

It's simple for your mood to drop and for you to feel worse than normal when there's a lot of strain on and emotions running high. Your capacity for self-control will be put to the test if this occurs. A lot of people find it difficult to maintain their discipline throughout difficult circumstances.

The Importance of Resilience

Life is an exhilarating adventure with many highs and lows. We mentioned David Goggins, a former Navy SEAL, a few chapters back. This man is renowned for his extreme resilience, discipline, and mental fortitude. Goggins used to hold the record for the most pullups completed in a day. He pushed so hard on his 2012 first try at this record that a muscle actually broke through the flesh of his right arm. An x-ray taken subsequently verified that the muscle had also been ripped.

After barely two months, David was back at a pull-up bar, about to attempt and smash the record once more, despite this setback and the excruciating anguish it would have given him. He began again.

If most individuals had been injured twice in two months, they would have given up completely. Goggins waited for just two more months, which brought us to January 2013. This time, he accomplished 4,030 pull-ups in a 24-hour period, setting a new world record (for the moment).

David Goggins embodies resilience and toughness. He is a man who, mentally, will not concede defeat. In addition, he rejects giving in to despondency or weakness in the face of difficulty. He didn't really have much of an option. It took all of his mental and emotional fortitude to get him through his early years.

David had to go through the difficult experience of being separated from his elder brother after fleeing his father when he was eight years old. Furthermore, he relocated to an area that was nearly all white. As the KKK had its headquarters in this region as well, Goggins undoubtedly encountered a great deal of bigotry at school. Neither his professors nor anybody else seemed to care. Since he was the only black student there, his protests went unanswered, and the other students took advantage of him.

Because of the stress in his early life, David also started to struggle severely with learning. He stuttering and hair loss started even at such an early age.

Even one of these horrific occurrences would have caused many individuals all throughout the world to crumble and give up. They didn't even end there for David.

After growing up, he made the decision to enlist in the military with the hope of becoming a pararescue soldier in the future. Here, having to learn how to swim put his emotions to the test once more. David was terrified of the water and had never been able to afford swimming lessons.

At this moment, testing by medical professionals indicated that he was susceptible to sickle cell anemia. Goggins, who was intellectually and emotionally drained by his experiences, decided to give up and quit the army. His real cause was the

CHAPTER 9: EMOTIONS, FEAR, AND SETBACKS

sickle cell trait.

When questioned about his current situation, Goggins quickly acknowledges that he was taking the simple route. He acknowledges that he had the option to remain, to try harder, and perhaps even to fulfill his ambition of becoming a paratrooper. The true cause of his departure was not the medical diagnosis; rather, it was the growing anxiety and pain he was experiencing as a result of the swimming tasks and tests.

Goggins gained weight quickly when he was going through one of his lowest points. He got sick and fat and took a low-paying job as an exterminator. David Goggins, who was still grieving over his past, still dealing with bigotry, and going through one of his lowest times in life, came upon something that started a fire.

When asked about his present predicament, Goggins admits right away that he was doing the easy road. He admits that he had the choice to stay, to give it more effort, and maybe even to realize his dream of becoming a paratrooper. The real reason he left was not the medical diagnosis; rather, it had to do with the increasing agony and anxiety he was feeling from the swimming exercises and exams.

During one of his worst moments, Goggins put on weight rapidly. He chose a low-paying work as an exterminator after becoming ill and obese. David Goggins was going through one of his lowest points in life, still mourning over his past, still battling intolerance,

After suffering through life's little setbacks, Goggins made the decision that he would voluntarily endure severe professional setbacks. Throughout BUD/S camp and the remainder of Navy SEAL training, he would take it all in and suck it up. He knew this agony would pass, therefore he would put up with it. He was aware that by enduring this misery, he would be able to leave behind the daily misery he was currently experiencing. He understood that he would overcome the long-term suffering of his sad existence by putting up with the short-term hardship of training to become a SEAL. An actual example of emotional resilience is this man, who overcame horrific suffering to emerge stronger than before.

You need resilience as well as true discipline if you want to thrive in life. At some time, life will throw you a curveball and present you with an emotionally taxing circumstance.

A loved one might experience an unexpected event or your relationship could abruptly end. Every day, disasters occur all across the world, and their impacts affect everyone.

The worst thing you can do in these situations is react emotionally. You have to maintain your composure and goal-focused attitude.

Dealing With Emotional Reactions

Unexpected thoughts and emotions might both arise and throw off your discipline. Dwellings may arise from repressed feelings or anxieties. You may also experience intrusive thoughts, which appear to arise out of nowhere and appear randomly at random times.

You already know how to overcome these ideas; all you need to do is recognize and be conscious of them. When you resist them, they gain greater strength and your willpower is diminished, which leaves you with less for other tasks. Your willpower remains available for other things when you give in to them and then watch them. The notion loses force if you can give in to it and observe it objectively.

You are able to approach the idea rationally.

Though not precisely the same, emotions also function in a

CHAPTER 9: EMOTIONS, FEAR, AND SETBACKS

comparable manner.

Thoughts are purely random, emotions are typically the result of an experience of some type. While it is possible to experience emotions at random, this is typically an indication that something else is off; in most cases, intense emotions are being suppressed and held back. We make a lot of trouble for ourselves when we suppress and deny our feelings.

For the human body to function correctly, it has to be happy and healthy. If you are suppressing a great deal of stress or emotional trauma, it may start to show in unexpected ways. As a kid, David Goggins experienced toxic stress, which resulted in hair loss and skin pigmentation loss, as well as a stutter.

Humans struggle with emotions because we find the unpleasant ones to be unpleasant. We try not to think about them because we don't want to feel horrible, irate, or depressed. Though it doesn't always work, sometimes we are able to ignore them for a while without any serious warning signals emerging. Burying emotions also has the drawback that it is more difficult to keep things secret the more you bury. Your capacity to handle fresh emotional trauma diminishes as more and more emotional baggage accumulates within you.

Something may eventually erupt again without warning, resulting in a panic attack or collapse.

It doesn't matter how someone breaks; what counts is that they broke at all, and a major contributing factor to that breakup was the suppressed feelings that feed the breakdown.

You have to feel emotions before you can cope with them. This is a little different than permitting a thought since, when you experience an emotion, you will feel it completely, which is why some individuals choose to bury the feeling at first. Sometimes it's best to hide the feelings under the surface. You might need to put off unpleasant news until the end of a crucial meeting if it breaks while you're in the thick of it. In the field,

Though processing and feeling the emotion are still necessary, they should occur as soon as there is time and space available.

It can be quite difficult to feel emotions in this way, especially unpleasant ones. However, if you choose not to, the bad feeling will seep into your existence and impact you for the remainder of your days here on Earth.

It's best to just feel the emotion right now, completely, deeply. It will sometimes make you feel horrible, sad, and even furious at the world. However, there's a reason you feel this way; accept and go with it. Experiencing anger due to injustices in one's life is acceptable. Being depressed after a terrible event is OK.

This kind of experiencing your feelings will cause them to eventually fade. It's not necessary to make sense of what transpired; occasionally, horrible things happen to good people just as much as wonderful things happen to evil people. The world is devoid of laws and genuine explanations for why things occur as they do. That's how unpredictable life can be.

Processing emotions might take a lot longer than processing thoughts.

It just takes minutes to process a thought. Sometimes managing emotions only takes a few minutes. At times, they may require several hours, days, or even weeks. Everything relies on the intensity of the emotion and its underlying reason.

Some people will also experience emotions at odd moments in addition to life events; abrupt terror or anxiety are two examples. This typically has to do with suppressing feelings, not processing them, or not being conscious of one's own emotional condition. Additionally, meditation helps you recognize when you're about to enter an emotional state by calming you down.

In those cases, what you really need to identify and comprehend is the underlying trauma. It is up to you to discover what you have hidden and why.

After that, you may start to process the emotional trauma there and begin to unleash that sensation inside of you.

Processing an emotion requires feeling it, regardless of whether it is brought on by something new or something that has always been there. Sort through those that can be sorted through and discard the others.

Recognize and embrace the sensations you are experiencing as legitimate.

After then, you may let go of the feeling and resume your normal activities.

It becomes more difficult for you to experience emotional distress in the future if you learn to manage your emotions in this way. When you're extremely adept at handling your emotions, most things won't affect you that much. You'll be able to digest your feelings over time and be able to dismiss them in a healthy way in the near term.

Emotional Fuel

More powerful feelings (like the death scenario) will be harder for us to let go of fully. You process the emotion at this point until the majority of its intensity is gone. If someone were to pass away, you would process it until you were able to resume your normal life. Years may pass before you really realize that this individual is no longer in your life, and that's okay.

Long-lasting emotions, however, can be employed in diverse contexts.

They can be sufficiently digested so as not to harm us, and then they can serve as fuel for your practice.

You may experience wrath or rage as a result of unpleasant

feelings and experiences. You have the option to direct this and utilize it to strengthen your discipline. Many military members have told me how their motivation to succeed in life comes from thinking about their buddies who are no longer with us. They utilize the fact that they have close relatives who are no longer with us as motivation to live life to the fullest and accomplish all that they can. Some people have extraordinary motivation that is fueled by the passing of family members, especially parents. Whether or not their loved ones are still with them, these folks are doing all in their power to make them proud.

It's risky to act on this raw passion since it might drive you in unpredictable directions. It may cause you to act rashly and needlessly in perilous situations. It is best to give the emotion as much thought as you can. Given that I have experienced some negative things in my life, I personally employ this technique. Like a lot of individuals, I've gone through difficult times and unexpectedly lost several family members. I was able to control my emotions to the point that I was no longer depressed or furious with everyone or anything. I worked through them till I could function, but the events that had occurred still caused me to feel slowly smoldering rage.

I gaze at this slow-burning rage.

In a similar manner, positive emotions can also function. Envisioning the life you desire and the joy you may experience. If you are in a relationship, you can see the benefits your discipline will bring to both of you. Consider the additional time you two may have if you practice mental discipline and become financially independent.

This is also applicable to happy memories from the past.

You may psychologically link the benefits of good encounters to your sustained mental discipline. You might use them as a benchmark or objective to work toward while you do your everyday duties. Emotions, both good and bad, can combine to produce extremely high drive. Positive energy works better for certain people than negative energy does for others.

You have much more motivation to maintain discipline if you can tie a goal directly to the good or bad things that have happened in your life. When something profoundly touches you, it might be difficult to let go completely. You'll probably remember it even though you can accept and digest it. Do you recall what I said before about how I feed off of my own bad emotions?

You are able to follow suit.

Use the discomfort, stress, or difficult moments you have gone through in life as fuel for your path. Make the most of your sense of being teased to motivate you to get a new body. Make use of the terrible experiences you've had to fuel your drive for achievement,

Emotional Toughness

You also become less sensitive as a result of feeling emotions and allowing them to be fully experienced. People who instantly bury their feelings never truly experience them. They decide the anguish or pain is too great and bury the emotion, giving it no attention at all. The bad emotions will affect you less the following time if you decide to experience these feelings instead of ignoring them. You grow more resilient and capable of handling difficult circumstances.

The goal of emotional toughness is to allow emotions to surface in order to develop resistance and resilience, not to suppress them. Because your thoughts originate from the logical component of your body, the brain, they are much easier to deal with. Usually, they make sense.

Emotions are not like that. They are illogical since they originate from your feelings. They typically come from an uncontrollable location outside of your body as well. Random things happen in life all the time, and some of them will always be negative. Recall that life is like a roller coaster, with just as many ups as downs. Even in the absence of the negative events, happiness would be unattainable for you.

Imagine a youngster that grows up in a rich and protected environment. They seldom ever had any negative experiences. They eventually go through a breakup or a terrible social rejection, let's say when they are teenagers.

This would be a far more intense sense of loss and suffering than they have ever experienced.

In contrast, consider a youngster from a third-world nation who has seen constant conflict. This child won't be as negatively impacted if, by the time they reach adolescence, they have moved to a safer location and go through the same breakup. They can probably move on from the breakup and deal with it in a healthy way because they have previously suffered much worse lows than this one. Joy is also far more accessible to this person. For this person, simply having access to food, drink, clothes, and shelter along with safety in daily life would be extremely beneficial.

However, the spoilt kid in the previous case wouldn't truly cherish such items. They could even take the pleasures for granted because they would already be accustomed to life's necessities.

Regardless of how good or awful something has happened, we must always acknowledge that it has happened. We then have to deal with it and live with it. Some emotions, such as the grief of losing someone, may be used to our benefit if we can channel them into fuel. However, some emotions will always leave us feeling hurt or sad about what went wrong.

This typically occurs when we are having trouble determining the cause. Why would something like this occur? Why to you or to someone you really love? The short response is that there isn't a clear-cut explanation. We don't always get clear answers in life.

Even while emotions might be painful, you don't have to let them rule your life or how things turn out. You may maintain your discipline and be depressed at the same time. Demonstrating emotional resilience is demonstrating to life that you will not back down from your goals, especially in the face of hardships encountered along the way. It is quite uncommon for someone to embark on any meaningful life path without suffering. The individual who can keep going forward in the face of adversity, even if they need to take a quick break or slow down temporarily, is more important. But never completely stray from the road.

10

Chapter 10: Overcoming Fears and Setbacks

When it comes to discipline, identifying what is preventing you and why is crucial. Many of the most significant issues people have with mental discipline are internal, stemming from the thoughts they release from their heads.

Negative thinking, intrusive thoughts, and low self-esteem are all mental health issues. However, they are not the result of your thinking. There is a fear, uncertainty, or lack of confidence at the root of the problem. You start to mistrust your abilities or yourself as a result of these issues. Not only will it be unclear why these ideas are occurring to you, but your motivations will be distinct from those of others.

I began delving more into self-analysis at this point. Since I genuinely wanted to succeed and be in control of everything on the outside, I was curious to learn what was actually going on behind the surface. According to my study, there are a few typical worries that prevent people from reaching their full potential. Have you ever had the overwhelming feeling that you ought to or even truly want to accomplish something, but

CHAPTER 10: OVERCOMING FEARS AND SETBACKS

you can't seem to get started? Have you ever had plenty of time to do a task only to realize that you're working slowly, not really attempting to focus, and eventually it's almost too late?

It seems strange, as like you aren't truly in control of yourself.

However, a lot of individuals have noticed this trend, and some of them have done extensive research on it. They have discovered the mechanism and underlying ideas that underlie these phobias by penetrating deeply into the human psyche. They've learned which anxieties are typical for most individuals by doing that.

Common Causes of Self-Sabotage

Here are some of your worst worries, along with the body, mind, and soul logic behind them. Keep in mind that the issues arise not from the fear itself, but rather from this perception and reasoning.

Reason is able to disprove these preconceived notions. Logic allows you to realize that these emotions are based on doubt and negativity rather than reality.

Please take note that not every phobia on this list is shared by every living person; some individuals will always have different wiring. The following are the typical profound anxieties that people have:

- Fear of Change: Achievement could bring about change. Try as you would, success might bring about change. People view change as difficult, sometimes harmful, and unpleasant. And who can predict what it will truly transform into? Perhaps it's best to continue living the life you already know.
- Fear of Responsibility: You can be given additional duties if you perform well in life. It's possible that you'll have to

decide on far more significant matters or take on greater responsibility. Being there might be rather stressful, particularly if you make a mistake! Perhaps it would be best to stay away from everything and focus only on taking care of yourself.
- Fear of Expectation/Pressure: When you begin to excel or perform well, others may look on you to continue in that manner. What happens if you are unable? Even while the concept of excelling and being excellent in anything could appeal to your mind, maintaining that level of performance for the remainder of your life seems difficult, exhausting, and lengthy. After all, success sometimes seems ephemeral. You just make a new mark and have to repeat the process when you reach a certain point. Perhaps it would be easier to just remain out of all that and find a peaceful, safe place to be. That way, you know, no one can expect anything from you?
- anxiety of Not Being Good Enough: This anxiety is typically fueled by society. It's a fear of failing and appearing awful in front of people or of realizing you're not as good as you thought you were.The fact is, everyone has setbacks occasionally. Being awful at anything is normal, which is why we need to grow and get experience. You begin to improve with time and have the potential to be successful. It can be difficult to start at all if your initial worry of failing is due to a fear of ridicule or anything similar. In this instance, you're choosing to avoid trying because you associate failure with such intense suffering.
- Fear of Attention: Not everyone enjoys being the focus of attention. Their goal is to blend in. There are proverbs like "the nail that sticks out gets hammered" and "the

tallest blade of grass gets cut first." These proverbs speak to this anxiety by implying that you will become the target of someone if you stand out too much. That is possible, but it is unlikely to occur to this degree. There won't be many Steve Jobss and Elon Musks in this world, let's face it. We don't have to be for the majority of us. Among a population of well over 7 billion, we do not have to be among the select few most well-known individuals to achieve our full potential.

- Fear of Ridicule: This fear is related to pressure and attention phobias. You have undoubtedly witnessed comedians being heckled by the audience at some time. Perhaps you have even witnessed an off-stage booing of a speaker or artist of any kind. These events are common in life, yet they don't mean the end of the world. It's simply an indication that something has to change and that you must adjust. Unfortunately, some people won't even attempt because they are so terrified of being told they aren't good enough. If pursuing your aspirations requires you to hear some hurtful remarks, perhaps it would be best to quit up.
- Fear of Ego: Some individuals fear success because they believe it will transform them. This results from a lack of self-confidence. Naturally, if you were given unrestricted wealth and authority right now, you might easily become corrupted over time. You tend to value things much more when you have to work hard for them. The reason that those with the most authority also possess the greatest responsibility is that they are the most capable of making wise judgments. They wouldn't have arrived at that point in the first place if they weren't. This also applies to you. Traveling to your destination will impart knowledge and transform you, but in a positive way.

- Fear of Overload: Compared to the other fears, this one makes more sense. It stems from a lack of confidence in oneself, which implies that there is little faith in the journey's completion and its reward. It occurs when you are already sacrificing things in other aspects of your life, like as your social or familial relationships, in an effort to achieve in life. The task would increase and your time will be more restricted if you succeed, right? Not really. You'll probably get to a point when you're content and stop striving for ever-greater professional success in favor of making life more enjoyable, unless you actually want to be Branson or Elon. You are aware of your objectives and needs.
- Fear of Change in Society This fear, which is similar to the fear of ego, is that success will alter your life. This time, the other people in your life are more important than self-confidence and power abuse. This dread frequently stems from a sense of alienation or loneliness. You get the impression that others will be left behind and that you will be traveling alone because you feel disconnected. The fact is that whether you change or not, some people will inevitably leave your life since you will always have people come and go. Pushing yourself through, nevertheless, will put you in a position to assist those around you. You serve as an example for them as well.
- A fear of falling short There are moments when the dread is of achieving and obtaining your desired outcome. It won't live up to your expectations, and you still won't be happy—it won't have really changed how you feel—is the concern. It's similar to the adage "money doesn't make you happy," but it applies to every aspect of your achievement. Money may offer you a lot of freedom to live the life you desire rather

than the one you have to, even though it can't, of course, make you happy. It can also provide you with a plethora of possibilities that you would not otherwise have. Why wouldn't you desire these advantages? It extends beyond financial gain as well, since success may take many different forms.

Setbacks

There are other challenges in the way of achievement than fears. Not everything goes as planned, so occasionally there may be setbacks.

Occasionally, the plan needs to be adjusted, and a setback serves as a helpful nudge in the correct direction. Dealing with setbacks that are tied to work is easy, but occasionally there are other causes behind them. Sometimes the issue isn't with your relationship, health, or other areas. You will inevitably run against sporadic, unpredictable challenges in life.

These issues have the power to ruin you if you allow them. When something awful occurs, it's simple to get into a pessimistic frame of mind or emotional condition. In these circumstances,

All that stands between you and your aspirations are obstacles in the form of setbacks. If you wish to go to the destination, you must conquer them. They are the cause of the majority of people's unwillingness to persevere and their tendency to give up before you. Recall your optimistic self-perception: you are a doer who creates your own luck. As much as possible, brush aside any setbacks and carry pushing onward.

11

PART 2

We've spoken about controlling your thoughts, which is a fantastic method to sharpen your intellect. We've also spoken about the value of emotions and overcoming adversity in life. To keep discipline, you need to take charge of these two areas. Willpower is the gasoline that drives discipline; self-belief and an analytical approach are the foundation that launch your discipline. Making a detailed strategy can help you navigate the world of mental discipline. This puts the "blueprint" to rest.

We'll look at additional useful advice for enhancing and preserving your mental discipline in this second section.

Chapter 11: How to Maximize Your Willpower

Some of the fundamentals of willpower were discussed in the first section.

One crucial one is that your willpower is finite and you have to make good use of it. Another is that by forming habits, you can take a slight shortcut. In addition, you have the ability to raise it, which we shall examine today in further depth. Momentum may influence this in both positive and negative ways.

Cognitive Fatigue and the Willpower Gauge

Mind weariness is also known as cognitive fatigue. Your brain experiences fatigue just like every other muscle in your body does. You have a lot of different things to pay attention to during the day. You have a lot to consider, notice, and absorb, whether it be from your personal or professional life. All of this fatigues and wears down your intellect. People find it more difficult to study in the evening since their brains have already expended a lot of energy. People are less able to do mental activities after vigorous exercise since their brains are also affected by low energy and overall weariness.

I have personally witnessed the impacts of this.

An illustration of cognitive exhaustion is this. For the kind of athlete who can effortlessly execute eight or ten different move combinations when they are first starting, remembering a series of four movements has become challenging. Your capacity to assess a situation or any information is compromised by cognitive weariness. It influences how you perceive issues and the kinds of solutions you are able to devise. Additionally, fatigue impairs your ability to make decisions; weary individuals tend to make worse choices than they otherwise would.

It's important to avoid cognitive tiredness and maintain mental clarity in order to maintain discipline and avoid making poor judgments.

The issue is that it's difficult to prevent cognitive tiredness. It would be like to advising an athlete that in order to perform at their peak, they must remain fresh.

One concept that is connected to cognitive tiredness is decision fatigue. This hypothesis states that every choice you make during the day depletes a portion of your ability to make decisions. Simple choices like what to dress, where to eat, and which order to do activities in all need you to use up decision-making fuel. Cognitive and decision weariness are associated with each other. Cognitive weariness impairs decision-making, and cognitive fatigue is ultimately caused by having to make too many judgments.

We have already discussed the willpower gauge and how each day's supply is limited. The willpower gauge, cognitive weariness, and decision fatigue are closely related to one another. Low on one tends to have a significant impact on the others.

It is quite hard to maintain discipline when one's mental energy is depleted and their willpower gauge is empty. There are several ways to handle this. The first thing to do is make your willpower gauge larger. Although we've already reviewed this section, let's review it quickly. The other two strategies are recharging strategies, which can assist temporarily top off your gauge, and willpower management strategies, which can help your willpower endure longer.

Increasing Overall Willpower and Mental Capacity

Increasing your general willpower takes time. Willpower is like any other portion of the body; it gets stronger with continuous use.

Your level of willpower will naturally increase as you start to apply discipline on a regular basis. Maintaining a generally healthy lifestyle can also assist strengthen one's will.

Let's use the example of diet. Poor eating habits might have an impact on your ability to maintain willpower. Allow me to demonstrate. Let's start with the assumption that you don't follow a schedule when it comes to eating, which means you don't give it any thought. You now have to actively choose what to eat and when to eat it. These two choices both slightly impair your capacity to make judgments.

You thus somewhat deplete your willpower tank with two options. Giving in to temptation when it comes to your eating choices also knocks your momentum, increasing the likelihood that you'll make poor choices later on. Due to the lack of a timetable, you may also return to work later than usual and work more slowly, both of which are poor choices that may weaken your resolve even more.

Conversely, there is the individual who follows a timetable and eats on time; the schedule need not be precise; it only has to be exact enough for them to know when to eat and when to return to work.

There's less consideration because the choice of what to eat has already been made.

Consuming wholesome foods also contributes to the stability and wellness of your body. It's critical to ensure that you avoid cravings, sugar crashes, and other unpleasant emotions. A certain amount of clean energy and vitamins and minerals are also necessary for your body to remain healthy. To maintain optimal physical and mental health, include all of this in your diet. It gets simpler to maintain discipline in this way.

Maintaining a balanced diet is beneficial for discipline and will generally make you feel better. A happy, healthy person has more energy, attention, and a better mood than an unhealthy one, which translates into a lot more willpower.

Willpower is linked to both mindfulness and meditation in the same way.

Additionally, you'll have a more balanced emotional state, and your body will only benefit from the cortisol reduction that has been shown to occur. It resembles the beginning of a positive spiral that affects every point covered in this article.

A healthy diet and practicing mindfulness may both help you feel better and have more willpower. This will empower you to make better decisions, which in turn will help you live a better, healthier life. This will also help you become more disciplined and form more positive habits.

Another excellent method to strengthen your willpower overall is to exercise. Exercise is important for your overall health in two ways: first, it relieves stress like no other. Your overall well-being will benefit your willpower. Along with burning some energy through targeted activity,

Numerous training modalities also maintain mental acuity without too taxing the mind. Your regular energy levels will rise with time, and you may also experience favorable mood changes.

Workout intensity helps you become accustomed to operating under pressure. This is an excellent technique for strengthening willpower, and special forces units all throughout the world employ it. Every unit I've heard of has a rigorous physical selection procedure that takes a long time.

Since no one will ever be fit enough to pass these exams, it isn't really relevant whether they are or aren't. They are made to push everyone to the very edge and keep them there, leaving them feeling worn out, agitated, and wounded all the time. In order to endure,

Willpower Management

Developing your general willpower is a process that takes time and yields few gains. Learning how to handle what you currently have is another approach to increase its quantity. Assume for the moment that your car's fuel tank and your willpower tank are identical. To yet, our main goal has been to increase our fuel capacity by purchasing a larger tank. But what if we also increased the engine's efficiency? In this manner, the automobile would travel longer on the same size tank.

Making the most of what you already have is a major life lesson. Everyone, for instance, have unique abilities. Each of us has likes and dislikes, as well as strengths and limitations. There aren't many qualities.

The individuals that are successful are the ones who maximize their innate attributes. A person with exceptional mathematical skills may use this ability to achieve their goals in life.

Someone else may be an athletic beast who, through hard effort and talent, becomes a professional athlete. Someone else may possess exceptional people skills and concentrate on building businesses and teams around those abilities.

Utilizing and maximizing what you have is what life is all about. An further example that comes to mind is Richard Branson. The Virgin brand was founded and is owned by Branson. Although he is today regarded as a prosperous businessman and billionaire,

Anyone who has followed Virgin would also be aware of the company's numerous business disasters. Nevertheless, the company continues to make enormous revenues and enjoy global popularity. Why? Is it because Brandon is a fantastic businessman in every way? Though you would believe otherwise. Rather, he is a man who is aware of his advantages and disadvantages.

He makes the most of his advantages (such as his superb marketing and leadership skills) and delegated his weaknesses to other experts. In spite of having the same 24-hour workday as everyone else, he manages to supervise the Virgin empire. How often do you hear people lament that they "don't have time" for something? The key to living a successful life is balancing your talents and weaknesses,

You may use willpower and make the most of your day by adopting the same mentality. Recall that increasing an engine's efficiency will prolong the fuel's life. So how can one strengthen their willpower more effectively?

First, make advantage of routines and habits. We've previously talked about some of this. Repetition makes a habit stick, and thus doing the habit seems more natural than not doing it. You are now conserving willpower, as the true expenditure of willpower would arise from deviating from routine and refraining from the habit. You maintain your willpower if you persevere.

Additionally, using the proper order is crucial. This relates to being aware of your own talents and flaws. Some people find that momentum is crucial, therefore they would rather start small and work their way up to the most difficult activities. Some like to take on the most difficult tasks first, get them done, and then move on with the belief that things will become easier during the day. For my part, I take a different tack. I prefer to "warm up" and gain some momentum with one or two simpler activities. I find it simpler to do the challenging things following this. Despite my knowledge that I am most productive in the mornings, I still prefer to finish the most difficult things in the early part of the day. Then, the chores get simpler.

Willpower Recovery

A healthy lifestyle for willpower restoration has previously been discussed, but a few key points were left out. We spoke about nutrition, exercise, and relaxation. For anyone who would like further information on relaxation techniques such as meditation, I have prepared several comprehensive stand-alone manuals. We shall now also discuss sleep in more depth.

Getting enough sleep is essential for preserving mental clarity. High levels of discipline will enable you to operate efficiently even when you're exhausted. However, you must first develop that degree of discipline, which is much simpler when you get enough sleep.

Sleep should always come first. If it's not an emergency, getting enough of sleep is preferable. Everything functions more effectively and gets done better when one is well-rested.

However, naps are also a good way to rejuvenate oneself and regain some self-control during the day. Though this can vary somewhat, humans typically sleep in cycles of ninety minutes. It's likely that you woke up during the deep sleep phase of your sleep cycle, which is when most people wake up feeling quite foggy and find it difficult to get moving for a time. Because of these cycles, you should aim to snooze for 15 to 25 minutes (to avoid falling too far into a cycle) or for about 90 minutes (to get a full cycle). Your body will frequently do a "fast cycle," which is equivalent to a 90-minute cycle in around 15 minutes, if it is really exhausted.

One approach to give your meter a little recharge is to nap. Taking a pause to have a snack or do some light exercise is another strategy. Make sure to completely disconnect from your daily routine and take advantage of this 15–20 minute break. After this, you'll feel better and be more concentrated.

Another technique for recharging willpower is meditation.

CHAPTER 11: HOW TO MAXIMIZE YOUR WILLPOWER

You might also try alternative techniques like sound therapy and hypnosis.

13

Chapter 12: Creating a Positive Self

CHAPTER 12: CREATING A POSITIVE SELF

Would you assume that a man wearing rags and reeking of foul air, resting on a park bench, was a diligent and successful man?

Now assume that you have just turned over in bed after waking up and seen that the time is 11 a.m. You gently stand up to see your room disorganized and full of random items. You require a shower, a shave, and a haircut. All of your garments require washing. You didn't even get out of bed yesterday, which is why the duvet is stained and there are filthy plates all over the place.

How are you going to clean up this mess and yourself first?

Or do you simply postpone it?

Now assume that you have just turned over in bed after waking up and seen that the time is 11 a.m. You gently stand up to see your room disorganized and full of random items. You require a shower, a shave, and a haircut. All of your garments need to be washed. You didn't even get out of bed yesterday, which is why the duvet is stained and there are filthy plates all over the place.

How are you going to clean up this mess and yourself first?

Or do you just wait till later—perhaps even tomorrow—because it's practically afternoon already?

A negative perception stems not just from what other people view but also from your own perception and emotions.

Who Do You Want to Be?

I find human life to be fascinating. It manages to adapt and endure in nearly any situation. It is possible for someone to be born with every advantage in the world, including attractive appearance, athletic ability, a wealthy and influential family, and a fantastic upbringing among the greatest people.

However, occasionally they will still go completely insane and discard everything.

Conversely, some people have dreadful birth conditions and traumatic childhoods in war-torn nations. They experience severe trauma as children and grow up without a family, yet they nevertheless manage to do amazing things.

The idea is that your past experiences and present situation are irrelevant. Rich individuals can unexpectedly lose all they own, and impoverished people can unexpectedly become millions.

You must first identify the kind of life and objectives you wish to lead. The next step is to determine the kind of person that leads that life. Go deep into it; what is this person's thought process? How does their typical day-to-day existence unfold? What kinds of judgments do they make? What motivates them, and what is going on in their minds? All of them are patterns that you must follow.

You will ultimately own what that person has if you can behave in the same way as that person. Consider this: you can essentially build a firm with the same levels of creativity, productivity, and business acumen as Elon Musk if you can equal him in these areas. Since they are similar individuals, it makes sense.

Building Your New Self

It takes persistent work to create a new you, but that's good since it strengthens your mental fortitude. Imagine this new, disciplined version of yourself. Try to visualize the life you would have and the possibilities that would be accessible to you for a short period of time each day. Visualization is useful not just for drawing in what you desire, but also for molding yourself into a different person.

Make a simple list of all the things you need to accomplish in order to transform into the person you want to be. Everything ought to embody this character. Acting confidently is the first step towards being a confident person! That implies that you need not become into an extrovert,

Your words originate from your ideas, and your words from your deeds mold who you are. Body language is yet another crucial domain.

A powerful posture is one in which your shoulders are broad and raised, your back straight. You don't think I'm real? Take several deep breaths and try to stay that way for a few minutes. You must feel more self-assured now.

Slouching down will have the reverse effect of making you appear smaller. Glance at the ground and speak in a hesitant, trembling tone. You'll start feeling worse quite quickly. Resuming your upright posture, take a few confident steps, and speak up with confidence. Heck, feel free to yell a little! You'll experience an immediate surge in feel-good hormones and a true sense of confidence following this.

Don't let life's unfortunate circumstances derail your newfound self-confidence; instead, rise above them. Recall and concentrate on how the new you would respond. Mindfulness breaks are another useful tool for controlling your emotions and staying on target.

When handling negative situations, there are a few methods from NLP (Neuro-Linguistic Programming) that may be useful. Reframing is the first step. Let's imagine you were recently irritated or angry, but it wasn't serious enough to cause you to lose your composure. It may be an unpleasant day at work, a disagreement with your spouse, anything.

All you have to do is picture the scene exactly as it occurred. While imagining this and experimenting with it,

The dissociation technique is the second. Either a recollection of something that's upsetting you or an emotion you're having trouble with can be seen in this situation. Imagine that you are now seeing the scenario develop from outside of yourself. If the scene is far enough away from you to see the entire block, you are likely inside a structure. Can you see how nothing else is genuinely affected by your circumstances or feelings?

Zoom out even more so you can see the entire town, the entire nation, and finally, all the way into space. Is your situation changing or having an impact on anything? Now, almost fully zoom back in to view yourself once again. What is your current feeling about the memory/emotion?

Staying on Course

You have to keep up the metamorphosis after you've started. Being completely honest with oneself is crucial. NBA great Kobe Bryant declared himself to be "the 200th best player in the league" and that he "freaking sucks" during a rough stretch in the 2015–16 campaign. This was a reflection of his recent performances rather than a judgment on his skill as a player. Anyone may make mistakes and do things incorrectly.

It important that you correct it.

Monitor your progress on this transition at all times. Jot down your true level of discipline. Just be honest with yourself and momentarily ease up if you're pushing yourself too much and slipping off many times. When you plan, treat yourself;

Relentless work is the real road to long-lasting transformation. Make the necessary corrections to the areas where you are falling short. Look for areas where you may improve on your current level of performance and discipline.

Along with visualization, positive affirmations are a useful tool for reaffirming the new you. Sustain your efforts by maintaining a cheerful and optimistic attitude about yourself. When necessary, take breaks—even if they entail a little vacation. You will be more disciplined and productive the happier you are.

Recognize your motivations and the person you are. Make use

CHAPTER 12: CREATING A POSITIVE SELF

of this information to motivate a disciplined lifestyle.

14

Chapter 13: Hacking Your Way to Better Discipline

People in life are constantly searching for ways to cut corners. Human nature is to seek more from life, yet achieving such goals requires a great deal of discipline and work. Businesses profit greatly from the societal lethargy that permeates society. Shortcuts are frequently pushed in the health, fitness, and

CHAPTER 13: HACKING YOUR WAY TO BETTER DISCIPLINE

cosmetic sectors. Businesses provide diet plans, miracle cures, and a plethora of other quick fixes for success and attractiveness. Get-rich-quick schemes and frauds abound on the internet since this is another area where individuals are looking for short cuts.

In actuality, everyone is able to determine the truth. The majority of individuals are well aware that there is no quick way. Everyone would have taken it by now if there was, wouldn't they?

People occasionally become fortunate in life and discover a kind of "shortcut."

However, this is often not a positive thing. The saying "it's about the journey, not the destination" may not be familiar to you. When I originally heard this saying, I didn't really get its meaning, but it's a powerful one. I now see that the lessons you must acquire on your path to achievement are the main emphasis of this statement.

A person with low self-esteem may think that improving their physical appearance will make them happier. They probably feel a lot better when they accomplish that aim. Is it because of the way their bodies appear? Only partly, as they've also mastered the skill of projecting confidence while working.

In the corporate world, someone else can be exerting a lot of pressure. By putting together profitable transactions and making money, they succeed. Do they now have that money because they have acquired the skill to earn it, or are they in a better position because they already have it?

I have simply mentioned one key lesson that has benefited those folks in the case above. There are a ton of more lessons on every voyage.

Better nutrition management was necessary for the person to undergo the physical change. They must have developed the will to work hard during exercise in addition to self-motivation and self-discipline. The outcomes will be better the more effectively these teachings are applied. The businessperson will have improved their money management, risk management, deal-spotting, goal-setting, and goal-achieving skills. It is all of this that enables him or her to flourish and become more adept with money. The person in question would not be where they are now without these teachings.

The lottery is the ideal illustration of a life shortcut gone wrong. Most people think that if they were given $1 million or more, they would be financially secure for the rest of their lives. Lottery winners experience precisely this, yet over 70% of them go bankrupt. **70%!**

It occurs because they have never been taught how to handle their money sensibly. They don't know how to live within their means, maintain discipline, or make money work for them. It's similar to someone who has liposuction to shed pounds only to gradually gain it back; taking the easy route doesn't provide the critical knowledge required for real, long-term improvement.

It is imperative that you approach discipline with this in mind.

You must maintain your resolve and concentrate even in the face of the unavoidably difficult circumstances. There are lessons to be learnt along the road, so it's not something that can be handed to you. It's common to falter and fall off from time to time, but what matters is that you keep going in the long run. Aim for daily improvement, and the objective will inevitably be reached.

Although achieving great discipline cannot be hurried, there are several strategies that can keep you on the correct track or at least stop some of the detours that lead to failure and bad discipline.

Tips and Tricks

This is a short collection of essential suggestions to help you develop self- and mental-discipline. Even if some of them have already been discussed, they are all gathered here for your convenience so you may easily refer to the list.

- Form routines. One of the simplest methods to maintain discipline is to form habits. For instance, let's assume you want to start working out in the mornings but are having trouble getting out of bed and sticking with it. It will seem much more natural to get up at the same hour even on days off if you can push yourself to do it for 30 days with an aggressive approach. The secret is to stick with it every day until the habit takes hold! If you truly need or want to lie in the future, you can do so; just make sure it doesn't happen too often since it won't break your habit. The same method may be used to develop other routines and habits, such as a nightly ritual.
- Another simple trick to maintaining strong willpower is to make a timetable. Your mental energy is less depleted because you are spared from having to make choices and, more significantly, from having to resist temptation. Similar to habits, this frees up your will for other purposes. Schedules and habits are not the same thing since a habit is something you do almost daily. Making use of a timetable allows you to plan your day around regular activities and accomplish other objectives, such as expanding your network or working on a side project. Making a list of the duties helps you stay organized every day by taking some of the thought out of your preparation. You may arrange them all in order to eliminate one activity, or you can just list the chores for the

day.
- In relation to temptation, we wish to get rid of it as much as we can. We are all susceptible to temptation; when a chocolate bar is staring you in the face and it's late and you're hungry, it might be difficult to resist. If people don't purchase junk food, they can't overindulge in it. If they have a web filter installed for recreational websites, they are unable to use the internet to put off doing their work. These are a few ways you can rid yourself of temptation. Better selections will always be made if you can eliminate the negative options. This will help you maintain more discipline. If you are not going to have alcohol in your home, how can you frequently consume too much?
- Conversely, make the better choices easier to access.
- If you want to read more books instead of watching TV, remove the TV from your bedroom and place some books next to your bed. Do you wish to consume a healthy diet?
- Have a sufficient supply of healthful snacks on hand. Exercise more is required? Purchase some household tools so you can complete the task there! Make it as simple as you can to choose the "right" option since people tend to follow the route of least resistance. Meal prep, for instance, makes it much simpler to follow a nutritious plan because, at this point, choosing the proper meal is also the easiest option.
- Another little method I employ to support the wise choices is a system of incentives. Reward systems provide incentives for maintaining self-control and making wise choices. Selecting the appropriate incentives and the appropriate frequency is the difficult part. For instance, you will end yourself consuming a lot of junk food at the end of the week if you treat yourself to an unhealthy snack at night after eating

properly all day. Because your body will start to expect junk food on a regular basis, this will also interfere with your ability to follow a good eating pattern or habit. Alternatively, you may treat yourself to a present or use a night out as your reward for sticking to a healthy diet over the week.

- Having an accountability buddy can help you become more disciplined. Motivating others comes more naturally to most individuals than motivating oneself. This is a result of your ability to examine issues objectively from the outside. Similar to the dissociation NLP approach discussed in Chapter 12, it allows you to view the problem's facts free of any accompanying emotions. This manner, you may quite quickly come up with the appropriate answer and approach and suggest that course of action to your friend. One word of caution: make sure your accountability partner takes this as seriously as you do so that you can rely on them to make an effort and maintain focus. Your discipline is greatly impacted by your action-oriented nature.
- Unbelievably, many individuals make mistakes just because they overthink things! They spend so much mental energy debating what to accomplish first or which activity is crucial enough to complete right now that they neglect to complete the work at hand! We'll go into more detail about this in a few pages. In summary, it entails doing more rather than thinking. Go ahead and start working on anything you know has to be done right now.
- When preparing your objectives or timetable, avoid taking on more than you can handle. It just takes one mishap or one delay to start feeling pressured if your calendar is already too busy. Be thorough in your planning and keep in mind that mishaps and emergencies might occur. Long-term

success depends on maintaining a clear and healthy mental state, so take care of yourself by working at a consistent, sustainable pace.
- Setting lofty objectives is commendable, but it's equally critical to maintain realism. Finding the ideal balance in this situation should inspire you, drive you to accomplish your objective, and fire you up.
- It needs to be a challenging enough objective to keep you motivated in this manner. However, a goal that appears questionable from the start is something you don't want. That puts you in a bad mood, which depletes your energy. Remain optimistic and productive by ensuring that the objective is reachable if you can maintain focus for seventy to ninety-five percent of the time. The number you select need to be determined by your current level of disciplined accomplishment; you should constantly strive for greater numbers every year.

All Positivity, No Negativity

Take a hard look at the pointers and counsel provided thus far in this tutorial.

You'll notice that the good aspects are highlighted rather than the bad ones. I disagree with using penalties for not meeting objectives since it might lead to negative mental health. Anything negative that has an impact on your spirit or mind is harmful. Give yourself a reward when you succeed, but don't punish yourself when you don't meet your goals.

Your new, disciplined self will be built on a foundation of self-love and a positive self-image. To reach your objectives, you must have a positive self-image.

If you had access to the selection procedures for some of the

CHAPTER 13: HACKING YOUR WAY TO BETTER DISCIPLINE

special forces groups in the globe,

Most people will begin to think badly in the absence of feedback.

When hunger, exhaustion, and cold are taking their toll, it's so simple to start losing hope and spiral into self-doubt and negative thoughts. It is crucial to have a good attitude. Generally, mental toughness is what separates troops who pass these examinations from those who fail. The minds of those who survive are extraordinarily strong.

Even though your mindset isn't the strongest right now, you can work toward having one. Remind yourself that everyone is capable of the same things, and concentrate on maintaining the correct mentality. It will eventually come naturally to maintain your optimism in the face of adversity.

Self-care is a crucial component of this as well. Taking excellent care of oneself and maintaining your happiness are essential components of successful self-care. A life in balance is essential for this. Don't deny yourself the pleasure and stimulation of social interaction. When creating the "new you," bear this in mind. You should arrange time for leisure; it's just as vital as making time for exercise, rest, and healthy eating. You have to maintain the machine that creates the output in order to maintain a high level, right? In this instance, your discipline is the output and you are the machine.

Maintaining an activity journal might be useful in assessing how well your entire strategy is working mentally. Similarly, journaling about your emotions may be beneficial for the emotional aspect of self-care. There are two primary advantages to keeping a log: a short-term and long-term one. Being more conscious of your emotions is the immediate advantage. By dedicating a little period of time at the end of each day, you may improve your emotional intelligence. It might take many weeks of effort for those who are more emotionally blocked to even begin to tap into what's truly behind the surface. It's worth the work, so get going right now. Gaining greater awareness of your emotions enables you to manage them more effectively.

Long-term, you might review a log and begin to see trends in times when you have depression. Maintain your timetables and to-do lists so you may compare this to them and see what is bringing you down. Do you experience anxiety or pain when you have a lot on your plate? Do you feel as though you're experiencing ups and downs on a frequent basis? Do you have worse sensations when you neglect a certain aspect of your life, such as your food or exercise routine? This is all vital information.

Stay true to the facts and use a detached approach.

An honest assessment can help you identify areas for improvement, which will improve your performance and discipline.

Regarding self-care, it's also important to consider your long-term goals. There is a tiny group that simply wants to rule their community every day. The majority of individuals have a goal in mind, and their discipline serves to build that desired lifestyle. To live a happy, healthy, and productive life, there should always be some discipline in that lifestyle. Having said that, the majority of us genuinely want to have fun.

When you're planning your future, keep that in mind as well. If anything (like traveling, yoga, or tennis) is going to be a long-term component of your strategy, you may as well attempt to fit it in as soon as feasible.

15

Chapter 14: Applying Your Discipline

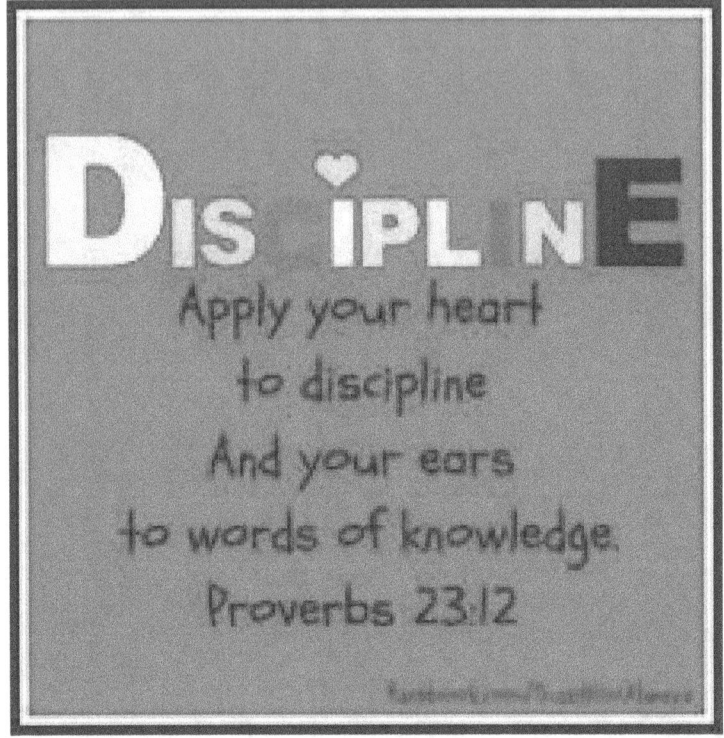

The previous chapter included advice on practicing mental discipline in the areas of preparation and planning. Making the most of your time and implementing those strategies are the main topics of this chapter.

The finest justification for discipline is summed up in a short saying by Jocko Willink.

"Discipline equals freedom."

Indeed, it is the primary motivator for people's intense pursuit of discipline. As a result of discipline, benefits grow. You can mold discipline into the kind of life you want. Now that you have the resources, the contacts, and the choices to live the life of your dreams, let's get started!

It is accurate, and the main motivation behind people's intense pursuit of discipline. Results and rewards are produced by discipline. Your life is shaped by discipline into what YOU desire it to be. Let's get started! Discipline provides you with the resources, opportunities, and relationships you need to live the life of your dreams.

Machine Management and Momentum

Every day presents a fresh challenge and a blank canvas to work with every morning. This is how you should always view your life. The fact that a fantastic, productive day advances you toward your objectives is the true prize. You should not feel the need to slack off because you are performing well; after all, your goals are your ultimate reward. That would actually be detrimental.

You will, of course, recall that we briefly discussed balance previously in the book. A happy, healthy person is more productive than an unhappy or stressed one, which is why balance is crucial. Take the necessary actions to ensure that this balance is maintained at all times. Treat yourself and maintain your happiness by using the reward systems.

You might as well make the most of your high level of happiness and morale by continuing to be active and disciplined. In this case, rewards are less significant since a motivated individual already performs effectively and doesn't require further motivation. Conversely, a dissatisfied individual may require a schedule that is less rigorous than normal as well as more incentives. Consider it as machine management and selecting the most effective strategy. When you're depressed, it's best to concentrate on taking care of yourself. You may start focusing more on the discipline aspect once your spirits are higher and you can manage pressure and setbacks a bit better.

Another advantage of starting every day again is that it motivates you to work more. Let's examine professional athletics as an illustration of this. There has always been an emphasis on a player's form, or recent performances, in professional sports. Every athlete, male or female, has the occasional very strong performance as well as poor ones. Even if they are regarded as the finest in their field, athletes may struggle for a period. When this occurs, they are either in a slump or have poor "form." An player who is playing above expectations and on a hot run would be the reverse.

Any athlete's expectations are predicated on their typical performance; a variety of factors, including skill level, motivation, and fitness, may come into play. It's not a science since different people react to the same problems in various ways based on a variety of factors, including beliefs, mental toughness and resilience, prior experiences, and more. An athlete may increase their odds of hot streaks and be less prone to slumps by practicing strong discipline, since some of these areas are also crucial for mental discipline.

Though they can occasionally result in overconfidence, hot streaks are beneficial for self-assurance and self-belief. When someone is on a hot streak, the issue arises because the fans and media become engrossed in it, living in the past, enjoying their success from yesterday, and taking it for granted. This is among the worst things that an athlete may possibly do. You must have the same determined attitude that an athlete has if you want to succeed in life. It's important to be able to control your ego and overconfidence, which might arise from achieving success. At the end of every day, week, or month, you must be able to start

CHAPTER 14: APPLYING YOUR DISCIPLINE

over.

In order to develop and learn from your victories, it's critical that you recognize and value them. They can positively inspire you and give you even more motivation. Just be careful not to take it easy on yourself while there is still work to be done and you are still pursuing your ultimate objective. It's hard to start again every morning for someone who is disciplined, on form, and pushing hard. It's an opportunity to work hard, establish your worth once more, and move closer to your objectives. This is the greatest method to capitalize on the momentum you already have;

Then, handling hot streaks seems quite simple, but what about slumps? Everywhere you look, there are always ups and downs. Nothing lasts forever; everything is always growing or shrinking, including businesses, sports, and even entire countries. Whatever term you choose to describe it—slump, rut, hole, or anything else—it all refers to a period of time when your performance has decreased and isn't up to par. This "standard" is what you have established for yourself based on your objectives, perception of yourself, and behavior.

It might be challenging to break out of a rut because of the opposite negative momentum. A rut will attempt to weaken your self-control and deplete your drive. In these dismal times, positive reinforcement and feedback are harder to come by, and you're supposed to work even harder to try to get away from them.

I want to stop thinking bad as soon as I can. Every roller coaster has to have its ups and downs, bad things happen, and there will unavoidably be challenging and easy times along the route.

An ancient proverb aptly summarizes these ideas. It says this:

"This too shall pass."

This is one of my favorite phrases for keeping your ego in check and your mind in balance, and it applies to both positive and terrible things. To overcome a slump, you must realize that overcoming the difficult portions of the path and learning how to deal with them has nothing to do with you or your deservingness of achievement. Keep in mind the lottery winners: if you reach your objective without gaining the crucial knowledge that will enable you to replicate the achievement if necessary, it will be for naught. Remain calm and inhale. Recognize that these are difficult times. Using the skills you've acquired, take control of your thoughts and feelings and begin transforming them into more positive beliefs.

You may have to deal with the impacts of poor mental health or feelings of powerlessness during truly difficult circumstances. Depression has the power to severely limit a person's life and perhaps send them into a downward cycle where they give up trying. You should consult a medical expert as soon as possible if any of these starts to occur.

Use the support system that is available to you; if you need emotional or mental help, turn to your close friends and family. Being quiet and powerful is a myth of the contemporary day. That refers back to the millennia of evolution that people have undergone.

We have always been gregarious, tribal creatures during those hundreds of years. Even today's indigenous groups that have eschewed technology and contemporary civilization continue to lead similar lives. These folks, as with all earlier humans, get together socially on a regular basis to talk about their lives and beliefs. People engage in straightforward discussions as a pack, airing out any issues and receiving closure and guidance on how they're feeling. It's almost like a kind of group therapy. Although maintaining a sound mental and emotional condition has always required this, throughout the past few centuries, it has been marginalized in contemporary culture. Numerous ideas exist as to why this occurred, some more bizarre than the others,

Working Through Tasks

It's all well and good to capitalize on or correct your momentum, but how do you really execute such things?

Chunking is the first method that will assist you in completing your timetable. Chunking is initially defined as a psychological method of learning. It entails dividing a large amount of information into smaller, easier-to-manage portions. Let's take the case of studying the Second World War, for instance. The narrative covers a wide range of events, from the years leading up to the conflict to their aftermath. Then there are the battles, the details of who fought when, and the how everything came together from 1939 to 1945. Attempting to retain all of this knowledge is challenging, particularly when seeing it as a single, large block.

You would divide it into smaller bits by chunking. You might concentrate on finding out what transpired year over year or according to the nations concerned. It doesn't matter which method you choose as long as you can divide material into manageable chunks that contain no more than five to eight pieces of information apiece. An individual's short-term memory can typically retain seven pieces of information at once. Before ingesting any more short-term knowledge, they must be sufficiently repeated to be stored in long-term memory. You will lose and forget the first seven bits of knowledge if you attempt to acquire more without first mastering them.

By breaking things down into digestible portions, you may not only learn more quickly but also increase your productivity. Here, chunking refers to a method for completing your chores or to-do list. Your goals should appear rather large and daunting when you look at them. We address this by breaking down each objective into manageable parts and concentrating entirely on the task at hand. You may apply the same method to chunking to solve any problem or task that is presented to you.

Assume for a moment that you need to thoroughly clean your home. It's a large task, and starting it might be challenging because you know there will be a lot .

Assume that your first task for the house cleaning is "cleaning the bedroom." That doesn't seem all that horrible, does it? If so, dissect it once again. Make your bed first, or maybe simply pull open the curtains. It's crucial that you take action as even a small move might build up some positive momentum. You will observe assignments being completed quite rapidly if you search around and attempt to do any minor work (five minutes or less) that you discover. You'll feel better too, thanks to the momentum, making it simpler to go on to the following section.

Your bedroom is ultimately taken care of by these small pieces, so you go on to another room and break.

Time, Intensity, and Action

In relation to five minutes or less, here's another useful tip to keep you focused and in control. Schedules and planners are excellent resources for you in creating the life you choose, but they may also work against you if you use them excessively. The instructions "take out the trash" and "brush your teeth" shouldn't need to be on the list. These are all routine duties

CHAPTER 14: APPLYING YOUR DISCIPLINE

that should be completed as soon as possible. Anything that can be completed in five minutes or less should be completed right away. If you allow these small tasks to accumulate, they may have an impact on your emotional and mental well-being. Instead, get rid of them right away to reduce your stress level and create the habits of acting quickly.

Speaking of quick action, our next piece of advice is called that.

The answer to improving or sustaining your mental state is to break up large chores into smaller ones, since this will make the work appear less daunting and time-consuming. Using this method makes getting started easier, because starting is the most crucial stage.

During my time in college, I occasionally had trouble with the larger homework. needing to write an essay that is ten or twenty thousand words long? Nobody that I've ever met has ever looked forward to a task like this. It can be a little scary even when you break it down into manageable portions since, regardless of the word count, a thousand or five thousand words still feels like a lot.

This is the optimal time for prompt action to be taken. You don't even have to bother about the ends or the pieces when you act immediately. You basically simply concentrate on getting started. 20 000 words to write? Fantastic, just go writing and see if you can write 100. Once you begin and write 100 words, you will most likely need to write more to complete your paragraph or the explanation of the topic. You could easily write several hundred words or maybe a thousand with this. This initial fervor will eventually subside, and your point will be established.

Recognize what to do at this point? Let's begin with the second point. Just get going, that's all. There are moments when you may appear and then quickly disappear, leaving.

During my time in university, I experienced periods of difficulty and had to "just start" every day, completing an assignment in around a thousand words each time. Sometimes, as soon as I started, I would get into a flow and the words would just come out of my fingertips into the computer. These were the days when I could accomplish more than half of my homework at once; on other occasions, I even completed the entire task in one sitting!

Getting started is an additional maneuver that utilizes the momentum concept. You have completed the hardest part of the process by starting: shifting from a position of inertia to forward motion. For the time being at least, it could be simpler to continue than to give up. You'd be shocked at how much this method can achieve. Try it out and make up your own mind!

The First Step

Because they place so much emphasis on it, most individuals find it difficult to take the initial step. Some people spend far too much time and energy making plans or choosing which things to complete in what sequence. Some people choose not to begin because they fear they won't produce their finest work. The worst thing you can do in either situation is to not begin. In the words of Mike Tyson:

"Until they take a punch to the face, everyone has a plan."

Iron This quotation alludes to how individuals would attempt to come up with a plan of action to cope with Mike, who is a legend. Formulating a plan is a smart move that may significantly improve your prospects in life. The issue arises when you formulate a plan without first experiencing the circumstance. The techniques that those who fought Mike Tyson were developing were predicated on fighting other individuals!

Since they had never sparred with Mike before, how could they possibly know if this would be a successful match? They didn't!

Put your attention on immersing yourself in the circumstance, getting going, and doing what you can. Sure, having a plan is a wonderful idea, but it may need to alter quickly.

It's crucial to realize that your plan could not work out on the first try, and once you realize this, it becomes far less crucial to come up with the ideal plan or approach before you begin. Keep in mind that even a careless, unplanned stride forward is preferable to the most meticulously planned move that hasn't yet occurred.

In addition, there is something known as the 40% rule. I originally learned about this from David Goggins, an ex-SEAL and all-around strong man. This is what he says:

In reality, you're usually only around 40% done when your body and mind tell you that you're done. The majority of folks give up there.

I was shocked to hear this at first, but it coincided with my decision to start taking my physical training seriously. Suddenly, I found it far more essential, and if enough other people felt the same way, I knew I could obtain the outcomes. At that time, I employed a trainer who had worked with several elite athletes.

Every day, I would wake up feeling like this person was cooked. During certain workouts, I was so tired that I looked at my trainer and begged for forgiveness, telling him I was at my limit. His reply? "I am aware.

Do this now. It was unbelievable! This person was assuring me it's alright that he understands I can't do this anymore. However, exert a bit more! I would attempt every time he begged for more, even though it was incredibly frustrating.

To be honest, I thought that after every push-up, I would fall flat on my face or that if I attempted a pull-up, I would slip off the bar. As it turned out, I would produce more one rep at a time. There were times when I didn't think I could complete the second.

These days, I'm aware that I have a lot more energy left in me even when I start to feel exhausted or depleted. It inspires me and strengthens my convictions so I can keep pushing a little bit harder, and typically that little amount is sufficient to accomplish my objectives.

Conversely, 40% of your attention and effort is most likely sufficient to advance as well. It all boils down to waiting for the ideal circumstance or scenario. It's just not possible for such things to occur, and improving doesn't require perfect form either. Generally, you can get things done if you can put in 40% of your effort.

Naturally, it's a good idea to hold yourself to a high standard and strive to produce excellent work. But in all likelihood, you won't need to produce your finest work very often. When it is, give it your all and concentrate on giving it your all. This is for those crucial, game-changing moments. You can survive on less than 100% of the time, and 40% seems to be the sweet spot where steady progress is made, work is reasonable, and pressure isn't too great.

Keeping It Interesting

Another thing you should do is take advantage of variation. Leading a disciplined life will occasionally need you to handle challenging or tedious chores. If everything was enjoyable and fascinating, discipline wouldn't be necessary in the first place. According to Jim Rohn:

CHAPTER 14: APPLYING YOUR DISCIPLINE

"The path to success is paved with discipline."

You must maintain your discipline to reach your objectives if you want to see them come true. The variety technique is one that enables you to persevere through difficult times and to keep going until the work is completed.

Assume you have eight hours of labor ahead of you, all of which will be identical tasks. Upon seeing this, some individuals could feel inspired to take it on head-on and finish all eight hours at once. First of all, this is not a clever method to approach this issue; it is a poor plan. For this task, the direct method is a very crude, brute force tactic. It might function, but most people won't find it easy to maintain.

Adding some variety to your day is a wiser approach to handle it. Divide the eight hours of work into eight one-hour work periods. Take a little pause to do something else in between each block.

A proper lunch break might be one of such breaks. Another may be a brief pause for meditation. Another would indicate that it's time for a little stroll or some exercise. You may squeeze in a variety of breaks, such as time for quiet, exercise, rest, eating, and socializing. Make every effort to maintain a high level of production. Research suggests that taking a short break, even just a few minutes to stroll about the room and clear your head, might be beneficial.

Try a few different break times to find what suits you best.

For the first several hours, I personally take a quick break every hour, generally lasting five minutes. I'll need a longer one after that, perhaps for lunch or some exercise, but this should last me for the next few hours. Then, as the end of the day approaches, there are a few more brief breaks before lengthier ones.

Try several things to determine what suits you the best. It's also a good idea to keep a diary of your performance using various break methods so you can see how productive you were with each set up, rather than assuming or basing it on how you're feeling.

By alternating between jobs, you may employ variance in another way.

There may be several distinct kinds of work listed on your daily schedule.

It is possible that you may have to perform some labor, some cleaning, and some administrative tasks. To avoid becoming trapped on one activity for more than a few hours at a time, you may create a timetable that alternates the amount of time you spend on each task. This maintains your motivation strong and your thinking fresh. Working on several things for a few hours at a time is far simpler than working on one activity for several hours at a time. Our brains are adapted to variety; they thrive on a variety of stimuli and can recognize and avoid .

Adaptation

We discussed adaptability a few pages ago when we discussed the Mike Tyson phrase, "Everyone has a plan." Starting with being ready to adjust your plans is a smart idea. This isn't because the plan isn't sound; rather, it's because circumstances change frequently and you never get the whole picture while preparing. Only when you are on the ground and acting do you get the whole picture. This is the time to identify the issues that require attention.

Setbacks are signals to adjust the strategy, not the objective, when you are moving forward. Maintain a positive self-image of yourself and never forget your disciplinary aim. Just as sports teams adapt their strategies to the situation, so do military groups.

CHAPTER 14: APPLYING YOUR DISCIPLINE

One can approach an issue using the same methods one does for everything else. Dissect it and determine which problem has to be solved first.

Concentrate on this initial task and figure out the answer, even if you have to try a few alternative approaches before you find the best one. Once the first problem is resolved, you may go on to the second and so on. This kind of thinking will enable you to acquire any skill.

The more difficulties you have to deal with now, the less they will effect you later on, thus experience will help you accomplish all of this even better in the future. It also helps with discipline. One more David Goggins quotation:

"Your brain needs to develop calluses in the same way that your hands do."

He is discussing overcoming difficult circumstances. Goggins engages in ultramarathons and a wide range of other insanely challenging activities in order to strengthen his intellect, which has encountered adversity on several occasions. He performs the things he detests under the most trying circumstances in order to be psychologically tough and self-disciplined in all circumstances. The benefits of discipline experience will be the same for you. It will fortify your mind and help you become accustomed to discipline, which will make it simpler for you to maintain discipline later on. It even enables you to strengthen and intensify your discipline. Keep in mind that this is a marathon, not a sprint, so you don't want to put too much pressure on yourself at the beginning. Better to have steady, ongoing development that will increase.

Chapter 15: Boosting Your Efforts

You ought to be able to significantly strengthen your mental discipline only by following the guidance provided in this article. You now possess the methods and resources necessary to live a more orderly life. We just completed discussing how you should

CHAPTER 15: BOOSTING YOUR EFFORTS

and can improve upon a disciplined life to make it even better. There are degrees to everything in life, and you may unlock the kind of life you desire by honing your discipline to the utmost degree.

It's simple to observe the various levels in sports. There are several sports teams at various levels and divisions. Some people excel in high school but find it difficult to succeed in anything else. Some persons succeed in reaching the professional level and are regarded as exceptional skills. Whatever your skill level, you can always get better. Cristiano Ronaldo is among the world's top soccer players. This 34-year-old player has been regarded as one of the finest since he was a youngster and is still producing at the highest level. Despite being considered one of the best of all time, he is renowned for his professional, disciplined approach and absurdly high work rate.

"I believe I've changed from the previous year. I'm constantly looking to get better at both my game and myself.

"I understand that I am the hardest person on myself, and that won't ever change."

This dude is obviously incredibly motivated. He isn't slowing down, even though he and Messi have been regarded as the finest players in the world for more than ten years. He's actually still working very hard to attempt to improve even more. His character has developed as he's aged, enabling him to become even more disciplined and professional.

It's a mindset that everyone ought to strive to adopt. The path forward is continual progress.

Keep this in mind when you use the methods I've taught you and strive toward your own objectives. It is possible to grow even further with a solid foundation of discipline and a grasp of those strategies.

True Control

Any moment might cause the mind to stray and spiral into unpleasant thoughts. It may also cause bothersome, ineffective ideas to arise. Your emotions can also react differently to various circumstances and might cause problems for you if you let an occurrence in your life bring you down. Now that you are aware of the optimal course of action, things are different. It will still be challenging at times, particularly the emotional part. A person might become seriously out of sync with life when some genuinely awful things happen. If you have had a truly awful or traumatic occurrence, give yourself time to recover and come to terms with what happened.

You may gain a great deal of control over your own thoughts and emotions by using the mental and emotional management strategies in this guide. After achieving that, you may go to the next level, which is comprehending the feelings and ideas of others.

Gaining insight into your own ideas, feelings, and psychology is beneficial when attempting to comprehend the emotions and thoughts of other people. You'll start to recognize people's mentalities. Interacting with someone who lacks a lot of self-belief or has a distracted mind may reveal these traits. This is a useful tool that helps you better understand and manage their thoughts and emotions by guiding them through them.

Why is it important that others maintain their discipline? because our environment has an impact on everyone of us. Maintaining discipline, happiness, and productivity will be much more difficult if you're surrounded by negative, unruly individuals. Conversely, surrounding yourself with disciplined and upbeat individuals can encourage you to keep up your standards and put in even more effort.

Positive effects on people are apparent to them as well. It will help you project a disciplined public image of yourself, which comes after developing a disciplined self-image. If you find that having a disciplined self-perception helps you maintain it, then increasing the social pressure from other people to see you that way will also be beneficial.

Your comprehension of your own feelings and ideas will also deepen. You'll be able to recognize symptoms early and will realize the moment anything isn't right. This aids in solving the issue more quickly and successfully. It becomes second nature to maintain a disciplined and upbeat attitude over time, so the focus is more on remaining on course than straying off course.

Maximizing Your Routines

It's time for you to assess your progress once more by doing some analysis. Although it's certainly simpler to determine where you need to make adjustments given your already high degree of discipline, keeping records and diaries is still highly beneficial. Seek for any holes or places where you can make even a tiny improvement.

Developing positive feedback loops to support your intended life objectives is also quite beneficial. For instance, you may reward your work-related discipline with fun fitness or vacation-related treats if your goals are to travel and get healthier while maintaining your work-related discipline. One way to treat oneself would be to learn a new recreational sport.

Receiving the award will have rejuvenated you and made you ready for work. The idea is that with the reward still fresh in your mind and providing extra motivation, you will be working even harder and maintaining discipline when you return to work (after your workout or after your vacation). You work even harder as a result, earning additional prizes, and so on, in a loop that continues until you achieve the greatest levels conceivable. You may exploit positive feedback loops in this way.

Remember the impact of momentum as well. Making the most of your progress means striking while the iron is hot. You should never let up once you are making progress and your discipline is becoming better.

A ball requires more energy to get rolling from a stop than it does to pick up speed once it is rolling. The same is true when discipline and momentum are combined. It shouldn't be too difficult to make a few more adjustments to become even more disciplined if you're already on the right track. Even a few easy steps might seem quite difficult to those who have no discipline at all.

Don't let your hard work go to waste by concentrating on the overall development of discipline. One should never be a slacker.

It's vital to remember that a sudden loss of discipline may indicate untreated mental or emotional problems. Verify that you are genuinely making every effort to address these issues and maintain the health of your body, mind, and spirit. Since there are connections between all three of these areas, you must grow in each to lead a happy life (and to be productive while upholding discipline).

Additionally, you must make your healthy routines and habits a permanent part of your life. An excellent method to do this is to connect them to significant moments in your day. Have a pleasant morning routine in place?

Make eating breakfast and brushing your teeth the last steps in that routine; you could even tie it to a beginning routine.

It is possible to anchor any habits, even though some are more difficult than others. All you need to do is be a bit more inventive when choosing your prompts and triggers, making sure they mesh well with your regular activities.

17

Chapter 16: Defending Your Discipline

> If You Always Defend Your Child's Mistakes, One Day You Will Hire A Lawyer To Defend His Mistake. Discipline Is Not Child Abuse!!!

CHAPTER 16: DEFENDING YOUR DISCIPLINE

I'd want to give you another quotation. This one has been credited to a number of individuals, but I originally heard it in an interview with a youthful, prosperous businesswoman. He discussed his work rate, output consistency, and the reason it had remained so high in spite of his numerous accomplishments in the years leading up to the interview.

"Your current success poses the biggest threat to your future success."

Most people ignore it because it is so very accurate. It all boils down to the distinction between motivation and drive. Motivation is ephemeral and transient. Sometimes people experience motivation, but eventually they lose it and go off course. Being motivated is another story. As Eric Thomas states:

"You will succeed when you desire it as much as you desire to breathe."

Being motivated equates to being fixated. It will resemble Cristiano Ronaldo persevering despite being the greatest already. It will be similar to Tom Brady, who was selected in the sixth round of the NFL draft all those years ago. Even members of his own squad passed this individual by before he had a chance. He had doubts from the beginning, which gave him the motivation to become the best in his sport. In 2001, Tom Brady's third season as a player, he captured his first Super Bowl victory. At this point, a lot of individuals would be tempted to give up. Tom wasn't. They repeated as winners in 2003 and 2004. In 2007, they enjoyed a flawless season, winning every game.

Brady was regarded as one of the greats going into the game. Along with the fame, money, and endorsement deals, he also had a supermodel girlfriend. This is where most people's discipline would start to crumble with success. In the face of so much ease and choice, maintaining discipline requires an iron will and genuine desire. Brady has led the Patriots to three more Super Bowl victories since then. He is still at the top of his game in his 40s, proving that his success did not derail him.

Never forget the reason you embarked on this adventure. Don't let ease cause your discipline to deteriorate. There should only be a forward march on discipline until your objectives are met and your strategy is finished.

"No slack at all." — Jocko Willink

Charting Your Progress

Those target lists and step-by-step plans are crucial for tracking your success as you proceed along the self-development route. By following a plan step-by-step, you can always observe your current situation. It is a good idea to have a separate checklist, for whatever reason, that outlines EVERY step of EVERY plan you have, regardless of the subject matter. You may use this as a kind of master list.

Mark a step as accomplished by checking it off. The goal is to progressively cross everything off the list; however, crossing everything off would indicate that you're not pushing yourself as hard as you should and that you're not being as disciplined as you should be.

It's time to revise the list when even one item on it starts to resemble completeness. Setting and revising objectives on a regular basis is essential to personal development. There is always more to be done, even if you are getting close to being the best in your profession.

There is always space for development, even for the best in history. Being the best version of yourself, not the best in relation to others, is the goal. If someone were to gain the title of greatest of all time, they should endeavor to close the gap as much as possible and hang onto it since it is a mantle that may

CHAPTER 16: DEFENDING YOUR DISCIPLINE

be handed on in the future.

You should be ambitious even in the early stages of developing your plans and objectives. Setting a larger overarching objective and working your way down from there is a smart idea. As soon as the large objective appears to be within reach, start considering even bigger and better ones. Aiming too close to the goal can sap your motivation and passion. Large objectives provide great inspiration and the strongest motivation to maintain your productivity and discipline.

Internal Focus Versus External Focus

The individuals we discussed, such as Cristiano Ronaldo and Tom Brady, are excellent illustrations of individuals with an inward concentration. Elon Musk and Bill Gates both have an internal concentration, which is necessary if you want to keep going after you've achieved success in your profession.

If you have an internal concentration, it indicates that you think you can control and direct your life. It's a mindset that says you are in charge of your own path as opposed to an external perspective where individuals think their destiny is determined by the things going on around them.

Individuals that are outside focused tend to be helpless, hapless, and waiting for a major break or other unusual events.

Having a true internal focus also entails having an internal results emphasis. This implies that tangible outcomes are not as important as they formerly were, and that your success is not determined by how much money you make or how many awards you receive. When you have an internal focus, your attention is on optimizing your own productivity. Even if you've already achieved your financial objectives and you know that you can be more productive and disciplined, you should still be moving forward at full speed.

In actuality, no one can ever fully reach their potential since, as you advance, you will also discover new avenues for growth and little adjustments to raise your performance. Maintaining discipline is essential for handling this procedure.

Everyone is motivated and seeks discipline for a reason; if you're here, you must have a purpose since those without a reason wouldn't even start looking. No matter how long the trip has taken or how much of it has been finished, never forget this.

You should constantly be aware of any suffering or difficulties from your past that continue to motivate you. If you find yourself getting too comfortable, go back to why you initially started. Some people are so determined to achieve and raise their family's level of living or prevent unfavorable conditions that they don't even think the incident ever happened. There may also be joyful explanations;

Keeping Your Vision Focused

You should consider more than just your motivations. Don't forget your objectives either. You have to aim higher and bigger each time they approach. Naturally, you don't always have to give your all to your financial or professional objectives; discipline is about more than just achieving money success. Making the most of every moment of your life is the definition of discipline. If your company or financial objectives are being met and you don't really need anything more, you may still apply that discipline to improve other aspects of your life.

You make the most of your time when you practice discipline. That implies that after you achieve a certain degree of success, you might start spending more time with your family and comfortably handle their financial demands. You have more time to focus on your own well-being, leisure, and taking pleasure in life as you want.

CHAPTER 16: DEFENDING YOUR DISCIPLINE

One can enjoy social gatherings, hobbies, and more. Work is only one aspect of discipline; another is knowing how to work HARD so that you may accomplish more of your WANT goals. It all comes down to living the life you desire.

But even the person who leads a simple life filled with family, friends, and activities ought to be aiming higher. He or she could make an effort

Maintain the efficacy of your fuel and your goals by using visualization. Experience the related feelings that support your continued mental fortitude and self-control. Consider your motivations and the objectives you have in mind.

"I would picture things happening to me." All it would do is cheer me up.

Visualization is effective with hard work. That is the matter at hand. You cannot simply go eat a hamburger after visualizing it." — Jim Carrey

While it's a good idea to imagine and envision your objectives, be careful that you're not only picturing them in an attempt to attract them. It's crucial to have self-belief and a success attitude; in order to succeed, you must believe that you are successful and disciplined. However, because you're envisioning it, it doesn't actually happen. It occurs because you live a life that reflects your belief that you are these things, including the decisions, labor, and sacrifices that go along with being that person.

In addition to the vision, you want to develop routines that support your motivation. Develop the practice of reviewing your accomplishments and assessing your most recent development. Sincerely assess oneself to get the most out .

Use routines that yield observable results, like exercising. Such visual outcomes are potent because they serve as continual reminders of the efforts you have already made to better yourself.

Dealing With Setbacks

The last issue you will have to combat with your discipline is the unavoidable setbacks. You will ultimately experience setbacks in one form or another; it is a universal experience. It can have to do with anything in your career or personal life. It may be a chance event that merely impacts you, or it might be a major catastrophe that impacts a whole community, industry, or family. There are several types of disasters.

They're also a serious mental toughness test.

Do you recall our conversation on self-care? It's critical to remember that. It matters that you be well and content since you are the machine. You have to give yourself the time you need to process a negative event. Certain circumstances unquestionably call for time off, such as.

Reaching your objectives and avoiding hardship need mental toughness and discipline. Everything helps, even if you're just making a small contribution. By maintaining an output of 20% or less, you will be able to complete the most crucial tasks. When difficult situations arise, deal with them in a way that suits you. Use techniques such as meditation if necessary. Large events are challenging to plan for due to the wide range of possible outcomes. But when it's all over, it will have made a huge difference if you had kept even slightly on course.

There will also be little issues that are simpler to handle.

For the more prevalent issues, there are several excellent methods that can support you.

Let's review what we covered in the guide earlier on reframing.

Your perception of the issue at hand is more likely to be the source of your sentiments and thoughts than the actual problem itself. We all have different perspectives, which is why you may perceive something as less of a problem (or more) than others do. These opinions stem from our life experiences and the lessons we've learnt thus far.

Reframing involves letting go of the previous perspective and changing how you see an issue. It will need a lot of vivid imagination to experience the scenario and the unfavorable emotions and ideas you connect with it.

Reinforce this several times a day when you first start, and repeat it quickly for five minutes or longer at a time while varying what's happening. You will become far less sensitive to the issues as a result. They lose control of the pessimistic attitude they once held and get confused between the actual thing and these ridiculous, made-up events by overloading their memory circuits with them. Since you now have a clean slate and an undefined state, you may tackle any circumstance or issue objectively and with a fact-based strategy.

An early mention of dissociation was made in the handbook. At this point, you consider your circumstances,

This kind of problem-solving approach clarifies solutions. You can see it as though you are offering advice to a friend or relative who is experiencing the same issue. Additionally, you have the option to enlarge the image to see the issue and your circumstances as only a little portion of the vast globe we live in.

It's doubtful that your issue will be more than a ripple on the ocean that is Earth unless it's a massive asteroid that is traveling directly at us or an imminent nuclear launch. Finding the silver lining in your situation helps you deal with it better, but viewing it from the outside eliminates your emotional responses and reactions, which have no place in a methodical approach.

Make it a regular habit to see issues and figure out solutions. Imagine that in order to go through life, you would stop at nothing and maintain a high standard of discipline. Imagine yourself succeeding and reaching your objectives. By putting everything into vivid visual form, you will increase your self-assurance and faith in your capacity to solve problems.

To increase their potency, you can combine all of this with positive affirmations.

Regarding the affirmation side, I find that watching and listening to positive podcasts and movies is quite beneficial. It's similar to being surrounded by optimistic people all day; for me, it's the closest thing to having mentors and friends like Tony Robbins, Jocko Willink, or Gary Vaynerchuck. Every day, I surround myself with positive affirmations and beliefs by watching videos. It doesn't even require me to set aside time in my day, and it keeps my discipline at an exceptionally high level. I take breaks from work, listen to my podcasts and affirmations in the vehicle, and even take a bath or shower.

I've already given you access to extensive mindfulness and meditation resources.

18

Outro

This book has taken me on quite the ride thus far, so thank you for persevering if you're still with me. A few more steps have been taken on the arduous path of discipline. During that period, we have examined the components of discipline, its mechanisms, and its adaptability.

As I did many years ago, those lessons begin with shifting your fundamental ideas about yourself. forming a new identity of the person you wish to be in your head and imposing it on yourself by little choices. For me, it began with my university morning rituals and progressed from there. I gained knowledge on how to break up tasks, work long days with a lesser production (but never none at all), and produce.

Since then, I've started to plan my life, manage my thoughts and feelings, and promote my own growth by leading a better lifestyle that incorporates socializing, exercise, a balanced diet, and relaxation.

It has also been helpful to go beyond of my comfort zone in other aspects of my life; in fact, expanding your boundaries generally has many advantages.

Recall that if you truly want to lead the lifestyle that comes with it, life may become anything you wish it to. I'm talking about the actual world, not the fantasy created by Hollywood in which wealthy people get to lounge around all day and dictate to others.

Lead a wholesome lifestyle and capitalize on the increases in energy and productivity that come from proper sleep, nutrition, and exercise. Make use of socializing and leisure to maintain your mental well-being. Step by step, strengthen your willpower and mental toughness along the way.

Keep in mind that this is a long-distance race rather than a sprint. You must progressively adjust if you want to stick with it long-term to avoid being overwhelmed. Practice self-control and start breaking your old, harmful behaviors.

Once more, go slowly if necessary. Avoid taking on too much. Your body and mind are integral components of the machine that is you, and for the highest chance of success, you need them to function at their best.

A new self starts to take shape as you grow. After then, it's time to tackle the planning head-on. As the master planner and builder of your own destiny, establish new routines and include more as you go. Establish such routines and get rid of any lingering flaws and poor habits. Start to truly control your ideas and feelings. Since this is the region most impacted by mental health and relaxation, food, exercise, and socialization all matter. Make careful to maintain a healthy diet since it's amazing how much a poor diet may impair hormone production and brain clarity. By employing the strategies, you may gradually strengthen your willpower and improve the way you utilize it.

Make sure you offer the new self a cause to stay and establish it as permanent as possible. Make use of the fun moments and prizes. Live life to the fullest and take advantage of whatever opportunity you may have out and about, whether it's going out to clubs or traveling to a far-off place. The purpose of life is to be enjoyed, and if you're content and getting rewards along the road, it will only motivate you to work even more. I wish you well on your travels. Many others have benefited from the techniques in this guide before you. You now own the information, and it is up to you to decide if you choose to follow them. Best wishes!

Before you leave, one final thing: Would you mind doing me a favor? I require your assistance! If you enjoy this book, would you kindly leave an honest review and share your experience on Amazon HERE? It will just take a minute (I'll be content with simply a single phrase!), but it will be of great assistance to me and unquestionably good karma. If you had any issues or didn't appreciate the book, don't hesitate to email me at contact@mindfulnessforsuccess.com with suggestions on how I can make it better so that my readers may get more value and information. I'm always trying to improve and provide more value to my books.

Regards and best of luck! I'm confident in you and sending you my best wishes for your new adventure!

WRITTEN BY :
Edric Cannon
THANK YOU
THE END

www.ingramcontent.com/pod-product-compliance
Lightning Source LLC
LaVergne TN
LVHW011947070526
838202LV00054B/4833